New Nations and Peoples

Brazil

Brazil

ANDREW MARSHALL

with 93 illustrations and 4 maps

New York
WALKER AND COMPANY

Contents

1   The Contrast and the Paradox

FLY FROM VENEZUELA on the northwestern border of Brazil overland down to Rio on the Atlantic coast, a distance of well over 2,000 miles, and you get a haunting sensation not just of the vastness of the place but of the emptiness. For long hours you look down on a still, green sea, a wilderness of forest and yellow-green swampland. As you leave central Brazil you fly over scrub-covered plains and jagged valleys and patches of dark red earth; yet none of this, not even the sight of a river winding across the scene below like a tarnished silver thread, obliterates the memory of that monotony of drab, matted greenness of the heart of Brazil. Roads in these vast backlands are rare and those you do see mean little more than trails, starting nowhere and ending nowhere. They are, in fact, mostly earth roads which become rivulets of mud during the rainy season and vanish in clouds of red dust when the rains have gone. To arrive in the world of civilization of the coast is a shock. After those interminable hours of flying over primeval wilderness, to land at one of Brazil's great cities is like coming out of the darkness into a blindingly lit room. Brazilians are proud, and justly so, of their cities, these great white concrete symbols of progress, these monuments to their new industrial age. There are not many of them but they are larger than almost any capital city in Europe; and certainly they are uncompromisingly modern, with their skyscrapers and towers of glass and skylines like miniature New Yorks.

Yet, in a sense, these cities, with their fringes of squalor, are false monuments. The great majority of Brazilians, in fact almost three-quarters of the country's estimated population in 1964 of almost eighty million people, live within 100 miles of the coast. While these cities on which the Brazilians lavish so much attention grow larger

7

and more splendid, vast regions of the interior, with their treasure of natural resources, remain deserts; and poverty is the lot of half Brazil's population.

Sheer size has always been Brazil's greatest handicap, but, as one soon begins to realize, not just from a geographical point of view. Admittedly, the problem of distances and often savagely difficult country has kept great parts of Brazil isolated from each other, not only physically but spiritually. Unlike the early immigrants to North America who regarded the unknown hinterland as a challenge, the Portuguese discoverers and the first settlers from Portugual of the sixteenth and seventeenth centuries were content to settle on the coast just as they had done in Africa. More than a century went by before any real attempt was made to explore the far interior, and it was only at the end of the nineteenth century, over 300 years after her discovery, that immigration from Europe, other than from Portugal, began to be encouraged.

This hesitation of the Portuguese to venture too far away from the sound of the sea has become a characteristic of even the present-day Brazilian. As Brazil's population steadily increased – today it is growing at the rate of over 3½ per cent a year, which is higher than in either China or India – this concentration of economic activity on the coast has brought about an increasing drift of the rural population to the towns. The phenomenon of underdeveloped countries, the over-expansion of urban centres, is also happening in Brazil on a grand scale. The cities are becoming far too big; public services, from power supplies to transport and sewage, are simply breaking down under the sheer weight of their growing population. To the Brazilians of the coast, and also now to many immigrants, the interior is a fearful and abandoned world.

Brazil prides herself on having an elaborate code of welfare and labour legislation which was first drawn up in the days of the Vargas régime back in the 1930s, and it was revolutionary legislation which earned Getulio Vargas one of his nicknames: 'Father of the Poor'. Yet much of this legislation still does not extend to the rural population. The Brazilian of the interior is a forgotten man, and in the minds of his more fortunate countrymen on the coast, almost a creature from another world. He therefore leaves the land and makes his way to the towns, even if it is only to carry bricks and mix more concrete or sweep the streets, and to go home at night to a reeking shanty town on the outskirts. Although he lives in the city, he does not belong to it. Nevertheless, he feels, at least for a time, less abandoned than he did in those lifeless, isolated communities he left behind. These 'refugees' from the land are adding to that growing number of people who, like them, also live in another world. They are the great mass of the 'other Brazilians', the poor and the under-privileged; and the patience, the almost philosophical apathy of these have-nots, is beginning to crack dangerously. This neglect of the land and of the population of the interior, this often glaring disparity of lots even in cities, is not peculiar to Brazil, it exists almost everywhere in Latin America; but in Brazil, as with so many other problems, it is on an infinitely bigger scale.

But the immensity of their country has also had a psychological effect on the Brazilians. They have become perhaps too complacent. A great many of them do realize the dangers which this unbalanced development is creating, but they are able to console themselves, as a succession of their governments seem to do, with the fact that Brazil is a very big place. There is always that vast, rich interior to fall back on; all that unexplored wealth of minerals and hydro-electric power, all those millions of acres of farming and forest lands waiting to be worked, some day. Brazilians have come to regard the interior rather as gilt-edged securities safely stored away in a bank deposit box. They are right, of course, it is something which will always guarantee their future; but they seem almost neurotically jealous of this wealth which lies idle in the ground. Although they lack the resources to explore much of it themselves, legislation has been carefully devised to prevent foreigners often from even investing capital in projects which could develop this wealth.

To many potential investors, Brazil's nationalistic policies must seem as exasperating as the cussedness of the dog curled up in the manger. But Brazilians are suspicious of foreigners, although individually they are not exactly xenophobic; it goes deeper than that and the reasons can be found in their history, even in relatively recent history. They have had sorry experiences of being exploited and betrayed, but not only by foreigners. Beneath the aplomb Brazilians have an often deep feeling of insecurity and when one gets to know them intimately, one realizes that many of them, even the most unexpected persons, also nurse a peculiar and surprising inferiority complex which can be endearing when one begins to understand it. They have a neurotic fear of being cheated and the belief persists that behind every foreign investment, and even offers of aid, particularly when they are backed by advice as to its employment, is a dark scheme to usurp their sovereignty. But to the ordinary Brazilian, the foreigner is just one symbol of the potential exploiter, a more adroit exploiter, perhaps. In the economic caste system which has developed Brazilians are almost as suspicious now of their own capitalists and of the landed aristocracy, of the man who has always lived in the big house.

And so Brazil remains the epitome of the underdeveloped country. Yet the Brazilians of the cities and even those who would seem to have little to be merry about are incurable optimists about the future. Whether this is genuine optimism now, or a lingering and peculiar kind of fatalism, is difficult to say. But Brazilians have a saying that the Almighty was born in Brazil so their future is surely being taken care of. At least it is a testimony to their apparently undying belief in the everlasting world of dreams, and they do seem to have developed almost a forced euphoria regarding the broader aspects of the periodic crises, the shaken confidence abroad, for example, which their unbalanced economy creates. The Brazilians, despite so many disenchantments, are still one of the gayest peoples in all Latin America, although the happy-go-lucky temperament is more marked in those parts of the country where the coloured element is stronger. Yet to most Brazilians, so it would seem, every day is Sunday, a day to celebrate because next week everything is going to be splendid; and, after all, they do have that consoling thought to cling to: *O Brasil é grande*; Brazil is big, so very big. The underlying aim of those who brought about the revolution of 1964 was to jerk Brazilians back to the world of reality.

It is all perhaps a gross simplification of the complexity and the

Political map of Latin America

paradox of the Brazilian character today, but he has become an extremely complicated individual. Like all South American countries, Brazil is a nation of immigrants, but infinitely more so. The Brazilian does not have that basic Indian ancestry which has moulded the features and the mentality of many of his neighbours. He has a far more mixed ancestry and with the added ingredient of Negro blood to an extent that other Latin Americans never had; and it was contributed by the slaves who were brought over in their hundreds of thousands during a period of over three centuries. Brazil was also the only Portuguese colony in all Latin America, even though the spiritual influence of the Portuguese in parts of Brazil was to become superseded to an extent that Spanish influence never was in Spanish America. As immigrants, they became a minority when the influx of immigration began at the turn of the nineteenth century. Nevertheless, the Portuguese seem to have left behind them so many features of their mentality and attitude to life, and a tolerance which can sometimes seem like laxity. But the Negroes, as they multiplied and intermarried, coloured the religious beliefs and have contributed far more to the characteristic traits of a very large section of Brazilians today, including that streak in their temperament which prompts the sudden emotional explosions or the giggle at the funeral. Brazil's history, too, has had its peculiarities, and one result of all this has been that the Brazilian is a very different person from all other Latin Americans. But then, place a southern Brazilian alongside one of his countrymen born and bred in the north, and again you would have two very different people, although they have developed a certain similarity of outlook; and it is not the usual difference such as you expect to find between northerners and southerners. These two Brazilians are not only racially different; in their intellectual development they are often generations apart.

The United States of Brazil, with an area of just over 3,287,000 square miles, is by far the largest and the most populated of the twenty Latin American republics. She is in fact the fifth largest country in the world. Brazil spreads over almost half of the South American continent; seven of the other nine South American republics and the three European possessions, the Guianas, touch her borders. Half of the inhabitants of the South American continent today are Brazilians and at the present rate of growth, by the end of the twentieth century she may have a population of over 200 million. Brazil comprises twenty-one states, with semi-autonomous governments, and most of them are larger than any country in Europe outside Russia. There are also five territories within her boundaries: Acre, Amapá, Guaporé, Rio Branco and the 29 square miles island of Fernando de Noronha, 300 miles off her northeastern coast. These are administered directly by the Federal government. The capital, Brasilia, constitutes a separate entity in itself.

Even the educated Brazilian often seems to lack a clear conception of the complexity of this subcontinent of a nation. The diversity of the country and of her people, the gaping contrast between the world of crowded cities and growing industrial centres rising like oases in the desert, and that other world of poverty and primitiveness which is the interior, are certainly hard to digest. Such contrasts are the pattern of most Latin American countries; but, once again, in Brazil they are on a larger scale and somehow seem more brazen. In the great backward hinterland region, which accounts for almost two-thirds of Brazil, an area as large as Western Europe, the density of population is barely eight per square mile. Yet only a few hours away by air from this empty wilderness stand those modern cities like Rio de Janeiro, São Paulo and Belo Horizonte. São Paulo is four times the size of Paris; Rio de Janeiro, spreading inland through the valleys and along a narrow strip between the mountains and the sea, has a population of over three million. It is larger than any of the cities in the United States of America with the exception of New York and Chicago; and the Brazilians are feverishly dumping rock and earth on the beaches and pulling down hills and sluicing them into the sea to make more space for a city which has burst its seams.

Although Brazil has some of the roughest country in the world, she does not have those terrible barriers of high mountains, those imprisoning walls of great areas like some of her neighbours, the Andean countries to the west. Her highest peaks are below 10,000 feet and the altitude of barely three per cent of her territory exceeds 3,000 feet. Lowlands with an altitude of less than 63 feet, including the Amazon basin, account for almost half of her total area. But it is thanks to her mountains that great areas of Brazil, although lying geographically in the torrid zone, are healthy and, from the point of view of climate, comfortable even for northern Europeans. The great Brazilian plateau, a tableland rising to 3,000 feet above the sea and crossed by two mountain ranges, covers five-eighths of the total area of the country. It is an area twelve times the size of the British Isles. This plateau, the tablelands of the states of Minas Gerais, São Paulo and Rio de Janeiro, is the most prosperous part of the country. Its eastern ridge, rising 2,600 feet behind Rio de Janeiro and Santos, culminates in the Serra do Mar, the coastal range which follows the Atlantic for nearly 1,000 miles. The narrow seaboard stretching from Cape São Roque in the northeast, southwards to Rio Grande do Sul, varies in width, disappearing altogether at points where the Serra do Mar rises straight from the Atlantic. As it stretches south-ward, the coastal belt widens into a broad, grassy plain. This is the cattle country of southern Brazil. The highest peak of the Serra do Mar is the 7,366-foot-high Pedra do Sino, 'Bell Rock', in the Organ mountains, a jagged, rocky chain which forms the uniquely beautiful background of Rio de Janeiro. In colonial days, the Serra do Mar was the one formidable barrier to the interior, and even today it is crossed by only three railways.

West of the Serra do Mar, in the Serra da Mantiqueira, is the 9,820-foot Itatiaia peak, the highest mountain in Brazil. Still farther inland, between the basins of the Tocantíns and the São Francisco rivers, towards central Brazil, is the Goiâna system, a vast region of tablelands and deep river valleys. It consists of an eastern range rising to 4,200 feet and a western range which forms the parting of the Paraná and Tocantíns-Araguaia river basins, rising at its highest point to 4,500 feet. The vastest plateau of this region is the wilderness of Amazonia covering the greater part of the states of Mato Grosso, Piauí, Goiás, most of southern Pará and parts of western Maranhão. North of the great Brazilian plateau, on the extreme northeast, are the Guiana Highlands, partly forested and partly stony desert; it is an isolated mountain system extending eastward from the Rio Negro and the Orinoco to the Atlantic.

These variations in altitude, prevailing winds and distance from the sea produce often radical differences in Brazil's climate, which ranges from tropical and sub-tropical in the Amazon basin and on her northern coast down to Santos, to temperate in large areas of the inland plateau. In the far south, frost occurs fairly regularly and snow is not unknown. This diversity of climate has obviously had a decisive influence in the development of different parts of the country. But an even more important factor is still the lack of transport in these different regions and the difficulty of communication between them and the rest of the country. A great part of Brazil is still virtually without any means of economic transport. In the whole country there are only some 24,000 miles of railways and less than 28,000 miles of roads, most of which are not even paved. About 90 per cent of these railways and 80 per cent of the roads are concentrated in a coastal belt roughly 300 miles wide.

Brazil's problems of communication are not just an engineering challenge; they are also on a continental scale. Even though two of the largest river systems in the world, the Amazon and the Plate, and six of the world's largest rivers, flow through her territory, their value as lines of inland communication is so often nullified by sand bars at their estuaries, great rapids and falls along their courses, and sharp seasonal drops in level. Although it is estimated that more than 30,000 miles of Brazil's rivers could be made navigable, regular steamer services ply only about 10,000 miles. Six of her main rivers, the Amazon, the Madeira, the São Francisco, the Tocantíns, the Parnaìba and the Paraná with their tributaries form a network of waterways in vast areas where little or no other means of transport exist. No river of consequence, however, with the exception of the São Francisco, runs down to her long eastern coastline.

Brazil's rivers, with their 680 often primitive ports, will probably continue to play their important, though far from adequate role for a long time to come, for want of anything better. The tributaries of the Amazon, the River of Death and the Xingú are still the only ways into parts of Brazil where even a small plane cannot find a clearing or firm ground on which to land. But her rivers do provide her with one of the greatest hydro-electric power potentials on earth;

15

a fact which the Brazilians only really began to realize some forty years ago.

Brazil also has one of the largest internal airways systems in the world and the aeroplane, which has become the country bus of the interior, has played almost as great a part as radio in penetrating the spiritual isolation of remote inland communities. But it is obviously not the answer to her tremendous problem of transport. Meanwhile, a solution of sorts continues to be the river and above all the coastal ships, and many of these were built before the First World War. Brazil has one of the longest coastlines of any country in the world. It stretches for almost 4,600 miles from Cape Orange on her frontier with French Guiana down to the borders of Uruguay. There are 130 natural harbours along this coast, of which 47 are seaports. The remainder lie in or near the mouths of rivers or in the lagoons in the southernmost tip of the country. Although many of them are ill-equipped to handle even coastal trade, most of the principal harbours of South America are to be found on the Brazilian coast; the ports of Santos and Rio de Janeiro are among the largest in the world.

2   The Two Brazils

FROM THE VIEWPOINT of the prosperity or the poverty of her people, it would seem that Brazil can be very simply divided in two. There is also a third world, that vast wilderness of the far interior, but it is almost an empty world as far as people are concerned. One has, perhaps, come to think of Brazil now as a country where prosperity has taken root on the coast and the frontiers of poverty begin a few hundred miles inland. But in fact she cannot be divided so simply; her poverty knows no boundaries. It exists in even the most developed coastal centres. In almost any of her great cities, a street even in a most fashionable district can end abruptly in a slum. On the outskirts of these cities are the shanty towns; like dejected encampments of some long and hopeless siege. Poverty is only one dividing line; the line which truly cuts Brazil in two runs from east to west and it has been drawn not only by nature, but by man. Ever since Brazilians achieved their independence and began to build a nation they have concentrated their efforts on an area south of that line. Climate and other natural factors obviously had a great deal to do with this choice. But the south is also where the majority of European immigrants settled and this part of the country could also be described as white Brazil. The towns of the south have their slums and shanty towns too, but those of the north are bigger and infinitely shabbier. The two Brazils are the north and the south.

The greatest area of poverty and backwardness starts just south of the Equator in the hot, swampy, thickly forested region of Amazonia, where the temperature varies little and rainfall can exceed 150 inches a year. Even during the drier months from July to October warm, moisture-sodden winds blow regularly through the Amazon valley. Brazil's great deposits of iron ore and manganese, which are among the largest and purest in the world, are to be found here. Oil is also believed to exist, but the extent of the wealth which lies hidden in these wilds is unknown. Much of this remote world of the Amazon has not yet even been accurately surveyed.

The Amazon and its tributaries, which are the life-lines of this region, also form the largest river system on earth. With its sources and affluents in Peru and Ecuador, it flows for 3,900 miles and drains an area of almost three million square miles. In its estuary, into which the Pará and Tocantíns rivers also empty their waters, the Island of Marajó is almost the size of Belgium. The muddy green river swirling into the Atlantic stains the sea for a hundred miles out, for it is estimated that the Amazon pours over $3\frac{1}{2}$ million cubic feet of water into the Atlantic every second and carries with it more than 100 million cubic feet of silt in twenty-four hours.

In this great wilderness of the north and northwest, in vast, still largely unexplored areas such as the state of Mato Grosso, over three times the size of Germany, which has become known as Brazil's 'Green Hell', the remnants of the Indian population still live in conditions which have not changed very much over the centuries. Here, there are still tribes which have had little or no contact with civilization and where the white man or a stranger can still meet with a sudden and savage death.

Over 900 miles up the Amazon on the Rio Negro stands Manáus, the capital of Brazil's largest state, Amazonas. Although it is two-thirds the size of the Congo, great areas are unpopulated. Manáus, with a population of 200,000, is the farthest up-river port in the world capable of accommodating ocean-going ships. It was once also the centre of Brazil's great rubber trade. In the early twentieth century, Brazil produced over half of the world's supply of raw rubber. The latex trees grew wild in Amazonia, but they were never cultivated and no attempt was made at preservation. When Asiatic rubber, the result of scientific cultivation, came on the market, Brazil's trade collapsed. The rubber which was to kill Brazil's rubber trade came from trees grown from seeds smuggled out of Brazil in

1876 by an Englishman. They were planted in the Royal Botanical Gardens at Kew and the young trees were shipped to Ceylon where they thrived and spread to the Malay States. In Manáus, the Opera House, faced with Italian marble and where Caruso once sang, the museums and the great mansions of the old rubber barons, all built during those boom days, still stand as derelict monuments to a time when this was a centre of culture as well as great wealth in the heart of some of the most primitive country in the world.

On the southern side of the Amazon estuary, on the river Pará, 90 miles from the sea, stands Belém, the capital of the state of Pará. About a quarter of the inhabitants of this whole state, which is not much smaller than Amazonas, is concentrated in Belém, which has a population of 300,000. Some 250 miles eastward along the coast lies the island capital of the state of Maranhão, the port of São Luis, and farther east still is Fortaleza, the capital of Ceará. Through these four ports flows the bulk of the cotton, the oilseeds, the hides and sisal, the nuts, the timber and the carnaúba wax of the Amazon valley and the far north. Some of the towns in this region, with their graceful squares, their tree-lined avenues and still retaining a great deal of eighteenth-century architecture, have a shabby charm and the feel in the air of a more leisurely age. You will no longer find this in the south. But then there is the poverty, the shacks built on stilts over the slime of waterlogged ground, the hovels in the back streets; and always that haunting feeling that the crouching wilderness is never far away.

The states of Piauí, Ceará, Rio Grande do Norte, Paraiba, Pernambuco, Alagôas, Sergipe and parts of Maranhão and Bahia form the great northern bulge of Brazil which faces the west coast of Africa, 1,700 miles away. This northeastern region has a humid, tropical climate on the coast with a regular rainfall which is swept by the trade winds. The interior is semi-arid and plagued by long and recurrent droughts. The rivers here are mainly torrential in the flood season and their course is often highly irregular. In times of drought many of them dry up completely. The São Francisco river, which rises in the south of Minas Gerais and runs for almost 2,000 miles in a sweeping curve to the sea at the boundary of the states of

Alagôas and Sergipe, is the longest river lying entirely within Brazil's borders. Old, wood-burning river boats which could have steamed straight out of the pages of Mark Twain still ply its lower reaches, but navigation is interrupted by the Paulo Afonso Falls, a 260-foot wall of water, almost 100 feet higher than Niagara. Navigation is still hindered by the seething rapids for several miles above the falls. A plan to open the São Francisco to larger craft by dredging and damming parts of the river to control its level is being carried out. It is part of the ambitious São Francisco valley development scheme for electrification, irrigation and road building in an area in the northeast almost three times the size of the British Isles. With the São Francisco as its artery and its heart in the power stations being built in the brush-covered country round the Paulo Afonso Falls, this plan could one day bring life to regions which for generations have remained barren and forgotten. It is a plan which, on a more modest scale, was first thought of in the 1920s, but like so many of Brazil's development plans it is being held up through lack of money.

Yet the drought region of the northeast, the Sertões, is one of the most distressed areas in the world. For generations its people, mainly subsistence farmers like most of the inhabitants of the Brazilian interior, have struggled to cope with the almost constant scarcity of water. The worst of the drought region covers a vast area of the interior of the northeast. Its inhabitants, almost entirely of mixed Portuguese and Indian descent, are a strange, unique people. They are known as the *flagedlados*, 'the castigated'. In good years they scratch a living from their smallholdings and breed scrawny cattle which they drive in herds in a continual search for pasture. When the drought sets in and the hot, dry winds from Africa scorch the earth, even when the streams and the waterholes begin to dry up, these people still cling fiercely to their land. For food they are often reduced to sharing with their cattle a wild, cactus-like scrub; by night they dig into the dry beds of the streams in a desperate search for water. The flagedlados only give up and start the long trek down to the coast and on to the towns and the plantations of the south when their cattle, too, begin to die. Then they become exposed to castigation of another sort. In the worst of the drought of 1958, about five per cent of the Brazilian budget was earmarked for relief in the northeast. Families were to receive a ration of food and the men the equivalent of 2 shillings or 25 cents a day. In some areas, however, it had become usual for a part of these relief wages, sometimes a quarter, to be held back by local administrators and labour con⁄tractors; some flagedlados employed on emergency irrigation work were paid in kind, in such things as brilliantine and plastic combs.

The northeast is devastated by drought at least once in every ten years. Prolonged dry periods in this drought cycle are not uncommon, but usually after about two years the rains begin to fall in December. Sometimes, however, the rains do not come. This happened in 1958. Towards the end of that year two million people were facing starva⁄tion. Most of the rest of Brazil seemed to have become almost inured to the recurrent tragedy in this remote part of the country, but in 1958 things were different. Formerly, in time of drought, when the flagedlados reached the towns they soon moved on in their thousands southwards to seek work in the coffee and cotton plantations, or as casual labourers in the towns, making the long journey on the decks of coastal steamers or packed in lorries which southerners have nick⁄named 'cockatoo perches'. Few of these people have any sort of identification papers; they are in the hands of the labour contractors, and the authorities seem to close their eyes to what happens to them. At times, the men only are taken to their final destination; by one pretext or another, their women and children are off⁄loaded on the way. In 1958 the flagedlados revolted. Instead of moving away to find work in the south, they began to raid the nearest towns, breaking into shops and houses in search of food. It was a minor revolution, but it did succeed in making a great many Brazilians realize for the first time what had been happening in the northeast for so long. In this northeastern bulge of land there are some twenty million people and a great deal of poverty. This situation does not only exist in the Sertões; although in this region, too, there is a wealth of natural resources as yet unexplored. Not unnaturally, it is here that the communists are concentrating their attention. Yet the inhabitants of the Sertões want very little and no Brazilian seems to have a greater love for his own particular corner of his country than the flagedlado. They may be driven away from their land by thirst and hunger, but at the first reports of rain in the northeast many of them go back to start again.

Natal, on the easterly hump of this northeastern bulge, with a population of nearly 100,000, is the capital and the principal port of Rio Grande do Norte. During the Second World War, at the time of the North African campaign, it was a US air base. Dakar, on the west coast of Africa, is less than 2,000 miles away. Some 20 miles south is the old port of Recife, the capital of Pernambuco. Built partly on an island, with its canals and bridges, it is described by fanciful northerners as the Venice of Brazil. It is the largest city in northern Brazil and has a population of almost 800,000. About 400 miles southwards is the great Bay of All Saints, the 400 square miles harbour of the even older port of São Salvador. With a population of about 600,000, it is the capital of the state of Bahia and one of the oldest cities in the western hemisphere.

Founded in 1549, São Salvador, more commonly known now simply as Bahia, was the first capital of Brazil. She remained the capital for 214 years until it was transferred to Rio de Janeiro in 1763. This region of the north was where the Portuguese discoverers landed in 1500, and it was one of the first parts of Brazil to be colonized. It is one of the few places in the country which is still a living museum of Brazil's colonial days. Here you can see the palaces, the forts and the elaborate baroque churches which the early Portuguese settlers built with marble and gilded timber from Portugal. Salvador is known as the city of churches and there are over seventy of them. There are also the remains of the Dutch occupation of this region in the seventeenth century. In other parts of the country so many of these vestiges of the past have been pulled down or left to nature to demolish, for Brazilians do not have much reverence for the past, and perhaps it is understandable. Even in Salvador, parts of the old town are disappearing. Both Salvador and Recife are the main outlets for the sugar, cotton, cocoa, piassava and hides of the northeast. The state of Bahia is still a centre of Brazil's cocoa and tobacco trades.

The farther south one travels from Salvador, the more one realizes

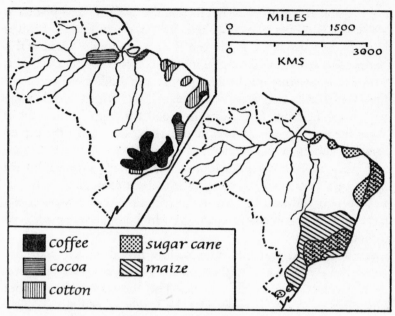

MILES
0   1500
0   3000
KMS

■ coffee   ▨ sugar cane
▤ cocoa   ▧ maize
▥ cotton

Map showing principal crops

that there are indeed two very different Brazils. One striking difference is in the colour of the people. The greatest concentration of pure
Negroes is to be found in the northerly coastal belt where there is not
only the look but the feel of Africa. But a great proportion of the
population of the coast as far south as Rio is noticeably negroid;
and here you will find a festiveness amid the squalor, for in its own
way this is also the gayest part of the country, with its carnivals and
often grotesque church festivals which last for days. Here, too, the
faiths and fetishisms which the slaves brought with them from
Africa still flourish; and they have seeped into the religious beliefs
even of the white Brazilians.

What has come to be regarded as southern Brazil is, in fact, a
relatively small area of the country. It comprises the greater part of
the states of Minas Gerais and Goiás, and Espirito Santo, Rio de
Janeiro, São Paulo, Paraná and Santa Catarina, down to Rio
Grande do Sul on the borders of Uruguay. While the coast is damp

23

and in parts almost tropical in climate, the cooler inland plateau is one of the healthiest parts of Brazil. The northern limit of frosts is found in the states of São Paulo and Paraná, and in the whole of this southeastern area the difference in seasons becomes accentuated. This is a country of vineyards, orange groves and cattle ranches, of tall pines and cotton and great coffee plantations which stretch away beyond the horizon. On a plateau 3,000 feet high in the state of Goiás the new capital, Brasilia, now stands. To transfer the capital from Rio 600 miles was condemned by more conservative Brazilians as a piece of extravagant madness. Yet perhaps inspired lunacy might be a better term, for Brasilia is the first attempt to break the magnetism of the coast by creating forcibly a new centre of attraction in the interior. But its cost is something which might have made even a Pharaoh blush.

Seven hundred and fifty miles southwards from São Salvador stands Rio de Janeiro, the 'Enchanted City', where every prospect pleases, except perhaps the climate. The hot season, from about November to April, is rather like the height of summer in New York, but it is due to the high degree of humidity rather than the actual temperature, which is deceptively moderate. During the drier months from May to October, there are times when the air has something of the feel of an English autumn. Brazilians have a saying that the Almighty made the world in six days and devoted Sunday to creating Rio; and its beauty is certainly breath-taking. Even though Rio, since April 1960, is no longer the capital and has become the state of Guanabara, it is still the spiritual capital of Brazil, a business, a political and a cultural centre and a Mecca for all Brazilians. Santos, 200 miles south of Rio de Janeiro, is the ocean gateway to the rich states of São Paulo and Minas Gerais. Most of Brazil's coffee and the raw materials for the factories of São Paulo and Minas Gerais pass through Santos, and in spite of over three miles of docks there is almost chronic congestion with long lines of ships anchored for days, sometimes weeks, waiting for a berth. Once a dreary dock town and a market-place for coffee brokers; a market-place which is one short street and which still handles the bulk of Brazil's coffee trade, Santos today, with a population of over 200,000, has been transformed into a seaside and residential suburb, a little Miami, for São Paulo, not much more than an hour away by road, inland over the Serra do Mar.

São Paulo, built on hilly country 2,600 feet above the sea, is one of the fastest growing cities in the world.[1] It has an often wildly erratic, but nevertheless one of the healthiest climates in the country and it claims the distinction of providing you with a variety of weather, from cold, misty mornings and hot noondays to tropical rainstorms and even hail in the evening, all in the course of a single day. Taking into account its surrounding municipalities, which are merging into each other, greater São Paulo in 1964 had an estimated population of over four million. In 1920 its population was less than 600,000. It is the manufacturing centre of Brazil; in fact, it is the largest industrial centre in all Latin America, producing almost everything, from razor-blades and motor-cars to sewing-machines and high-precision tools. Most of its larger factories have had the advantage of being built after the Second World War, and they are among the most modern in the world. It is a city of crisp, white skyscrapers and of almost aggressive prosperity where the will to work is your passport and your bank book becomes your visiting card. São Paulo has a horror of age. Stefan Zweig described it as a place where they pull down with alarming speed anything that recalls yesterday or the day before. *Paulistas* proudly point out to you that there are few buildings over eighty years old still standing. It is a city over four hundred years old without a wrinkle. It is also one of the most cosmopolitan places in Brazil and one of the most individual-istic, for the Paulistas still retain many of the ways of life of their immigrant forefathers. There are communities of Brazilian-born Japanese, Italian, Dutch, Middle Eastern, Swiss, German, Scandi-navian and British who seem so deeply proud of their city and state, and even of their weather, that they have never really been absorbed into the Brazilian mould. They even have a tendency to refer to other Brazilians in the third person. São Paulo is not just a place, it is an attitude; it is also the capital of the new Brazil.

The plateau region of the states of Minas Gerais, São Paulo and Rio de Janeiro, with its plentiful rainfall, good soil and healthy climate, has become, both agriculturally and industrially, the most developed part of the country; but here, too, there are great empty spaces. Over 35 per cent of the population of Brazil is concentrated in this region, although it accounts for little more than one-tenth of the area of the country. In the heart of this region, some 400 miles from the sea, stands Belo Horizonte. It is the only major city of the interior, apart from Brasilia and, like Brasilia, it was designed and built on a once empty plateau less than a hundred years ago. With a very mixed population of almost 600,000 in 1964, it is the capital of the state of Minas Gerais. Larger than France but with a population of less than nine million, Minas accounts for about half of Brazil's mineral production. It is also rich farming country and a growing industrial centre. Belo Horizonte is the only city in Brazil which the Paulistas grudgingly concede might one day be their rival.

Near Belo Horizonte, at Morro Velho, are the oldest gold mines in Brazil; they are also the deepest gold mines in the world. During the eighteenth century, Brazil was one of the greatest sources of gold; and the centre of this once fabulous industry still stands almost intact. It is the town of Ouro Prêto, 75 miles south of Belo Horizonte, and which was formerly the state capital of Minas Gerais. Gold is still mined in this region, but in latter years even richer deposits of iron-ore and manganese have been found. Much of the old town remains untouched, unreal, like a faded picture of the past. The steep cobbled streets, the splendid baroque churches and great monumental fountains built by the old gold masters; the houses in which they lived on the slopes of the hills surrounded by terraced gardens, with the slave quarters hidden by a line of trees, are still here. Ouro Prêto is the only place where the look of eighteenth-century Brazil has been officially enshrined. In 1933, the town was declared a national monument.

In this south and southeastern region of Brazil, rivers as well as climate have played an important role. Great stretches of the river Plate system which run southward to Buenos Aires, of which the three main rivers are the Paraná (the 'Mother of the Sea', as the Indians called it), the Paraguay and the Uruguay lie within this region. The Paraná river with its tributaries drains southwestern Minas Gerais and practically the whole of the states of Paraná and

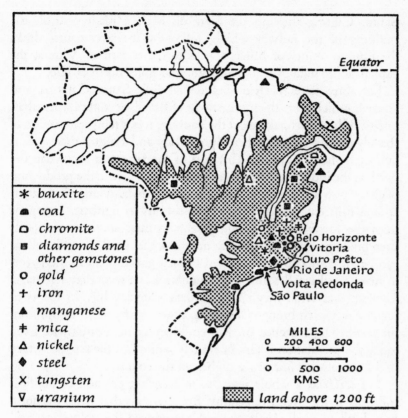

✳	bauxite
⬣	coal
▢	chromite
⬚	diamonds and other gemstones
○	gold
+	iron
▲	manganese
✦	mica
△	nickel
◆	steel
✕	tungsten
▽	uranium

MILES
0   200 400 600

0   500   1000
KMS

land above 1200 ft

Belo Horizonte
Vitoria
Ouro Prêto
Rio de Janeiro
Volta Redonda
São Paulo

Equator

Map showing mineral resources

São Paulo west of the Serra do Mar, as well as the southern parts of Mato Grosso and Goiás. Brazilian for over a third of its length of 2,500 miles, it is navigable for long stretches above and below the Sete Quedas falls on the Brazil–Paraguay border. The falls, with their eighteen cataracts, have a drop of 373 feet and they are one of the highest in the world. There are plans to harness over one hundred falls in this region for hydro-electric power. The Rio Doce, although only 138 miles of its lower reaches are navigable, has also played its part in the penetration of this part of the country. It rises in Minas Gerais and runs southeast to the sea through the state of Espirito

Santo. Cutting through the Serra do Mar, it made possible the building of the railway which, following the river course, links the iron-ore mines of Minas Gerais to the seaport of Vitoria, the capital of the state of Espirito Santo, 400 miles north of Rio.

The three states of Rio Grande do Sul, Santa Catarina and Paraná, which form the southerly tip of Brazil, account for less than one-twelfth of the total area of the country. It is a temperate region of sharply defined seasons where during July and August there is frost and even snow may fall. This part of the far south succeeded the north as the industrial centre of the country until, with the production of cheap power, São Paulo began to attract new and larger industries. It is as different from the rest of the country as northern Europe is from the Mediterranean. Immigration to these southern states has been predominantly German; so much so, that until the nationalistic campaign launched by a shocked Federal government in the 1930s, to many southern Brazilians, Portuguese was a secondary language. German was what they spoke in their everyday life. In the 1930 revolution which brought Vargas to power many of his troops from the south who marched on Rio could speak no Portuguese. Even today the population is almost entirely white and the rate of literacy in the far south is one of the highest in the country.

The south as a whole was also to have a great deal of political influence in the twentieth century. Brazilians say that while the north gave birth to intellectuals, the south produced the politicians; and the southern politicians, the descendants of the old 'political families', are still prominent in the Brazilian political scene. Pôrto Alégre, the capital of the state of Rio Grande do Sul, is also still an important industrial centre. With a population today of almost 600,000 it stands on the inner shore of a 116-mile-long lagoon, the Lagoa dos Patos, Duck Lagoon. At the entrance is Rio Grande, the largest port in the far south. Within the lagoon is yet a third port, Pelotas. From these and smaller ports along the southern coast come the beef, the hides, the wine, the canned meat and rice, the Paraná pinewood shipped to Europe and the coal from the mines of the south. These are the only coal deposits in Brazil, which help to feed the steel mills in the southeast, almost 1,000 miles away.

1 Part of the interior of the southern state of Espírito Santo, which is in sharp contrast to the equatorial north.

2 Much of the thickly forested and swampy regions of Amazonia in the north have never been accurately surveyed.

3 Lack of communications between the coast and the interior is being overcome by new road building; the new highway linking Belém on the northern coast with Brasilia in the southern interior.

4 Rio de Janeiro, Brazil's former capital, is surrounded by jagged peaks; this is Sugar Loaf Mountain at the entrance to Guanabara Bay.

5 Houses on stilts on the banks of the Rio Negro at Manáus, the centre of Brazil's once booming rubber trade.

6 Asiatic competition ruined Brazil's rubber trade. The marble-faced Opera House at Manáus stands as a memorial to the affluent days of the rubber barons.

7 In the Sertões region of the northeast subsistence farmers have struggled for generations with the problems of drought and poverty.

8 The old port of São Salvador, Brazil's first capital in the sixteenth century, is still a
principal port for the vast regions of the northeast.

São Paulo, the largest
industrial centre in Latin
America, symbolizes the prosperity of a new Brazil.

The São Francisco river is
almost 2,000 miles long. This
river boat is being unloaded at
Recife, in northeastern Brazil.

11 Ouro Prêto in the gold-mining country of Minas Gerais still retains its eighteenth-century look.

12 A *favela* or shanty town in Rio de Janeiro; such slums are often the blemishes on Brazil's modern skyscraper cities.

13 Carnival is part of the tradition, particularly of northern Brazilian life, for rich and poor alike.

14 The baroque buildings which remain in parts of Brazil are a heritage from the Portuguese colonizers of the sixteenth century.

15 Brazilians have little respect for the past; and even in historic Bahia parts of the old town are disappearing.

3   The Outline of the Past

WHEN ONE CONSIDERS the two social worlds of Brazil, these
two worlds of often brutal contrast where, in one, the struggle just
for survival is still the lot of so many people, it would seem reasonable
to suppose that Brazil has had a history to match the iniquities of
man and fate. Yet, looking at history you will find that every
momentous event, not only in her past but in modern times, too, has
come about in a singularly placid manner.[2] While her neighbours'
struggles to break away from Spain were marked by savage bitterness
and bloodshed, Brazil achieved independence from Portugal in the
early nineteenth century without a war; and it was proclaimed not
by a Brazilian but by a Portuguese, the son of the ruling King of
Portugal into the bargain. Unlike Mexico, the only other country in
the New World to have a king, Brazil's transition from a monarchy
to a republic in 1889 came about without violence and almost no
rancour remained between the members of the old order and the
implanters of the new. In fact, very soon afterwards Brazilians felt
a pang of guilt when they recalled the ignominious banishment of
that gentle, ageing man who had been their king from the age of
sixteen for forty-eight years.

The Portuguese on the whole were kindlier, or more lax administrators than the Spaniards, and Brazil – the only Portuguese colony
in all Latin America – saw little of the whiplash of domination and
the brutality which Spanish America witnessed; and generations of
Brazilians, although they do not always eschew violence on principle,
have developed a temperament that tends to shun mass, but especially
sustained violence. In this respect, too, Brazil's history is different
from that of most countries of the New World.

Discovered by the Portuguese in 1500, although the Spanish navigator, Vicente Yañez Pinzón had sailed up the Amazon earlier in the same year, Brazil remained a dominion of Portugal for 322 years. During this period the French established settlements in Brazil. For sixty years, at the time of the Spanish domination of Portugal, she became a colony of Spain; and for twenty-four years part of her northern coast was held by the Dutch. She was also the only colony in the world to become for a time the seat of the Empire to which she belonged. Brazil was one of the last countries in South America to achieve sovereignty. Her independence was proclaimed in 1822, when she was already a kingdom within the Portuguese Empire. Although Portugal withheld recognition of the New Empire for three years, thanks largely to the efforts of the British government she was persuaded not to embark on a colonial war over Brazil. Yet for her, the loss of this, her largest and richest dominion, was a final curtain on an era of discovery and empire building going back for almost 400 years.

In the sixteenth century, while Brazil still remained almost ignored by the Portuguese, the Spaniards were already busy exploring this new world of the Americas. In 1513, Ponce de Leon landed in Florida and Balboa first looked out over the Pacific at Panama. Cortés began the conquest of Mexico in 1519 and in the 1530s the Spanish were conquering Peru and Colombia. Towards the end of the fifteenth century Columbus had discovered Watling Island, Cuba and Haiti. In 1498 he had reached the mouth of the Orinoco. News of the discovery of America had caused bitter feelings in the Court of Dom João II of Portugal. The long rivalry between the two Iberian peoples who led the world in discovery might have erupted into war but for the intervention of Pope Alexander VI. Alexander proposed that the world be divided in two by a line drawn across the globe passing 100 leagues, roughly 300 nautical miles, west of Cape Verde Islands off the coast of Africa. Eastwards of the line would be Portugal's sphere of influence. Spain's domain would lie westward. In 1494, Portugal and Spain agreed to redraw the Pope's line. Under this treaty a line, which was to become known as the Tordesillas Line, was to pass 370 leagues farther west of Cape Verde, cutting through South America near where the town of Belém now stands at the mouth of the Amazon, down to Laguna in what is today the southern Brazilian state of Santa Catarina. In effect, a great part of Brazil's boundaries were drawn six years before the Portuguese actually discovered her.

How the Portuguese came to discover Brazil is still a matter of historical argument. Some say it was by chance when, in 1500, Pedro Alvares Cabral, a Portuguese admiral with a fleet of thirteen ships bound for India, veered too far westward off his course. On 22 April he sighted what he supposed was a great island. On shore he raised a cross cut from the trees and called the 'island' Vera Cruz. Later, after sailing for days up and down the coast, he renamed it Terra de Santa Cruz, Land of the Sacred Cross. There is also some doubt as to the exact spot where Cabral landed, but it is almost generally agreed that it was probably near what is today the small town of Pôrto Seguro in southern Bahia. How she came to change her name a third time – to Brazil – troubles historians too. It is believed that the name derives from a tropical dye wood the colour of glowing embers known since the Middle Ages, which also flourished in this region and which the Portuguese called *pau braza*. Others attribute the name to the legendary Island of Brazil which was believed to exist in the Atlantic. Venetian charts of 1436 gave the name of Isle de Brazi to one of the larger islands of the Azores. The familiar association of Brazil as the name of an island in these latitudes probably prompted early navigators to refer to the new land by the same name.

For over a quarter of a century Portugal seems to have failed to grasp the significance of her new possession. It seemed unimaginably wild, sparsely populated and apparently worthless, and the roaming Portuguese preferred the more profitable ventures in Africa and in the East. During that time, Portugal's rivals, especially the French, took almost impertinent advantage of this neglect. They set up trading posts and their ships returned laden with Brazilian woods; they even used the colony as a base to attack Portuguese ships returning from the Indies. In 1532, in an effort to establish some form of administration, Brazil's coastline was divided into fifteen fiefs, known as *capitanias*, which were granted by the Portuguese Crown, with hereditary rights, to favoured courtiers. The capitanias extended for 50 leagues along the coast and for an indefinite distance inland. The beneficiaries were given extensive rights and privileges, although the Crown held the right to levy export taxes and had the monopoly of trade in woods and spices. The system was a failure, for many owners never even took possession of their lands. Only two capitanias flourished, São Vicente, which was to become the state of São Paulo, and Pernambuco in the north, where the first sugar-cane plantations were introduced and which is still a centre of Brazil's sugar industry. These two capitanias were also to play a uniquely important role in the racial composition of Brazil, for they began the process of miscegenation in the colony. The ineffectuality of the system of capitanias which tended to divide rather than unite the colony, led to the establishment of a central form of government. The capitanias were gradually taken over by the Crown, either by pur-chase or because they had been abandoned by their original owners. By the end of the eighteenth century all the capitanias had reverted to the Crown.

In 1549, Tomé de Souza, a Portuguese nobleman who had earned fame as an administrator in India, was appointed the first Governor-General of the Brazils and São Salvador was chosen as the seat of government for the whole colony. While the original owners of the capitanias, or provinces as they were now called, were allowed to retain some of their rights, administrators directly answerable to the Governor were placed over them. Slowly the organization of the colony took shape and settlers began to arrive in steadily increasing numbers. Later, in 1572, the colony was divided for a time into two provinces, North and South, with capitals in São Salvador and Rio de Janeiro. It was only in 1763 that Rio was chosen to be the sole capital.

With the establishment of the central government the first attempts were made to bring some form of elementary culture to the colony. In this respect, too, Brazil was very much of a desert. There was no Indian civilization such as the Spaniards had found in Peru and Mexico. The Brazilian Indian was a primitive creature; even the more advanced tribes were at a very low level of development. The early Portuguese settlers had a primitiveness of their own. Although there were some dedicated colonizers among them, for the most part they were convicts, exiles and adventurers, and all of them had but one ambition: to make a quick fortune and get out. Even today, Brazilians will tell you wryly that that seems to have been the ambition of so many foreigners who came to Brazil even in the twentieth century. Those early settlers, fired by tales of the treasure hordes which the Spaniards were finding in the west of South America, believed that surely the same plunder was to be had here too. Yet it was over 190 years before anything like it was even found. Towards the end of the seventeenth century gold was discovered in south-eastern Brazil and in a region only some 400 miles from the coast. It set off the world's first great gold rush and in a sense it was a tragic discovery.

In 1549, when the first central government was established and Tomé de Souza arrived in São Salvador, seven Jesuit Fathers came with him. They were led by Manuel da Nóbrega who was to be one of a long line of missionaries dedicated to the conversion of the Indians to Christianity and to fighting for their protection from slavery. On both counts the missionaries were bitterly resented by the settlers but they did lay the foundations of education in the colony; and, rudimentary though it was, the Catholic Church was to be the only provider of education for almost three hundred years. Manuel da Nóbrega founded a school for the training of missionaries on the site where the city of São Paulo now stands. In the years that followed, some of the Jesuits started schools on the coast while others went inland to found mission communities where Indians were settled, and taught simple crafts and the rudiments of farming.

In 1574, the Jesuits won what was to turn out to be a dubious victory over the colonists. The Crown decreed that Indians converted and settled in villages were protected from slavery. The colonists were only allowed to enslave Indians captured in 'legitimate warfare'. As the colonists' interpretation of 'legitimate warfare' covered raids on mission villages where, thanks to the missionaries, the Indians had become reserves of sitting ducks for the slave hunters, the antagonism between settlers and the Jesuits grew even more bitter. But the Portuguese had always found the Indians unwilling and poor workers. They also had very little resistance to the white man's diseases and thousands died in captivity. This, much more than the restriction on Indian labour, led to a new form of servitude and on a far larger scale – the massive introduction of slaves from Africa.

Tomé de Souza had barely settled in office when the colony was faced with invasion. In 1555 Nicholas de Villegaignon, with only two ships, took possession of Rio de Janeiro Bay. He was followed soon afterwards by other ships bringing settlers. Although the Portuguese had first explored the bay on a New Year's Day fifty-three years earlier, unaccountably they had never occupied it. The French action was to have been the prelude to the establishment of a colony which according to the prime mover of the scheme, Villegaignon himself, would have offered asylum to the Huguenots and other Protestants. John Calvin had been persuaded to give the expedition his blessing. But Villegaignon was a clumsy colonizer and back in Europe the disillusioning news of his failure effectively discouraged immigration to this 'sanctuary in the New World'.

Twelve years later, in 1567, a Portuguese force blockaded Rio harbour and forced the French to surrender. The city of São Sebastião, which was to become Rio de Janeiro, was founded in the same year. Later the French founded settlements in northern Brazil from where they were not so easily dislodged because, unlike the Portuguese, the French had won the friendship and respect of the Indians. To this day, the capital of what is today the state of Maranhão, and where the French had settled in 1612, still retains the name of São Luis, for the French had named it Saint Louis after Louis XIII. It was only by a twist of fate that part of Brazil did not become a colony of France. France had never recognized the Tordesillas Line and the partitioning of the New World between the Spaniards and the Portuguese. Another part of northern Brazil might well have become a Dutch colony.

In 1580, Henrique of Portugal, the last of the Portuguese ruling dynasty, died, and Phillip II of Spain laid claim to the Portuguese throne. By intrigue followed up by invasion he made good his claim.

Brazil became a Spanish colony. Expansion towards the west and a gradual penetration of the interior began during these sixty years of Spanish rule. Brazil, as a Spanish colony, now lay open to attack by Spain's enemies. Chief among these were the English and the Dutch. In 1624 the Dutch attacked. A fleet financed by the Dutch West India Company took São Salvador, but they were forced to withdraw a year later. In 1630 the Dutch attacked again, this time in Pernambuco. It took them over five years to consolidate their position but by 1637 the Dutch seemed to be firmly entrenched. The Governor of New Holland, John Maurice of Nassau-Siegen, a Prince of the House of Orange, was a man of vision and, unlike so many of the Portuguese and Spanish administrators, he had a great sense of justice, and was also a man of culture. He brought to Brazil not only the first scientists and scholars but also Pieter Post, the architect, and his brother Frans whose Brazilian landscapes gave Europeans their first glimpse of what Brazil looked like.

Maurice's liberal plans to develop the colony, which included agreement with the Portuguese, might well have established the Dutch in Brazil. But the Dutch West India Company was more interested in expanding and tightening its hold, rather than in statesmanship. In 1644, Maurice resigned and the prestige which the Dutch had enjoyed disappeared with him. The revolt against the Dutch which very soon broke out was unique in so far that it was the initiative of the colonists. Lisbon was prepared to accept the presence of the Dutch but the colonists were not. Their revolt lasted for almost ten years and it was only in its latter stages that Portugal sent help. In 1654, Holland, too, lost her foothold in Brazil. Britain had an alliance with Portugal and although marauding English carried out raids on the northern coast of Brazil, loading their ships with tropical timber, and built forts and trading posts, they never made any attempt to follow the Dutch or the French in establishing settlements.

In 1640 Portugal regained her sovereignty from Spain, and Brazil was again a Portuguese colony. In São Paulo bands of settlers had been penetrating farther into the interior. Some of them had reached the banks of the Amazon and beyond. Others, going westward, had come to the Peruvian frontier, the Guaporé river on the border of Bolivia, and down to Paraguay in the southwest. These settlers roaming far into the wilds became known as *Bandeirantes*, the 'Flag Bearers'. The main object of their expeditions had been to capture Indians for slaves, and incidentally dislodge the Jesuits from their settlements, although a great many of these Bandeirantes were themselves part Indian and owed such emancipation as they had to the Jesuits.

The Bandeirantes were a primitive and often brutal people, but Brazilian history was later to record them not as barbarbic slave hunters or merely explorers. These men drew Brazil's boundaries to the south and the west and prevented the Spaniards from extending their domain northwards beyond the region of the river Plate. The Bandeirantes went far beyond the limits of Brazilian territory laid down by the Tordesillas Treaty; in fact, they laid claim to an area greater than the part of South America which had been apportioned to Portugal by that treaty. Some of their expeditions, veritable armies of people in which entire families took part, including the women and children, lasted for several years. To this day São Paulo takes pride in being referred to by the rest of Brazil as the capital of the Bandeirantes. In 1693 the Bandeirantes found gold in Minas Gerais.

News of the discovery electrified Portugal. In Brazil the colonists abandoned the coast and headed inland; new settlements sprang up in the wilds around the gold fields and in 1727 diamonds were found in the same area. Although this stampede opened up the interior as more settlers and an increasing stream of new arrivals from Portugal penetrated farther inland in search of new deposits, on the coast settlements were all but abandoned and the growing sugar industry in Pernambuco, which was the basis of Brazil's economy, practically collapsed. Portugal, heady with the prospect of the wealth which her new colony was at last yielding, imposed strict laws to increase production of gold and diamonds. The easygoing, often lax attitude of the Portuguese administration suddenly hardened. The mines, which became the monopoly of the Crown, were decreed forbidden territory and Indians and Negro slaves were driven to work as never before. In the frenzy to increase output from the mines, more slaves were brought in from Africa. The unpopularity of the Jesuits, fighting hard to protect the Indians from the slave hunters, smouldered into a hatred which years later was to cost them dearly.

In the latter half of the eighteenth century, the Marquis of Pombal, the autocratic Prime Minister of Portugal under King José I, introduced a series of sweeping reforms in the colony. The last remaining rights granted to the owners of the capitanias were revoked. The capital was transferred from São Salvador to Rio de Janeiro, immigration from Portugal and the Portuguese Atlantic Islands was encouraged, and Indians, at least legally, were given the same rights as whites. Incensed by the Jesuits' attempts to oppose some of his measures, particularly their refusal to accept any authority but their own over their settlements, Pombal banned the Jesuit Order not only in Brazil but in Portugal also. The colony had never forgiven the Jesuits for their protection of the Indians; some of their alleged commercial ventures, and the property the Order had acquired, had aroused deep resentment too. In 1760 the Jesuits were expelled from Brazil.

For years resentment against Portuguese rule had been growing. Since the early days of the colony, Portugal, deeply suspicious of her more powerful rivals, the English, the French, the Dutch and the Spaniards, had virtually isolated Brazil. Trade, if such it could be called, was a one-way channel to Portugal. Ports were closed to all but Portuguese ships. With the discovery of gold, the policy of economic suppression and isolation was intensified. Any kind of manufacturing enterprise was forbidden lest it compete with the mines for labour or with imported goods from Portugal. This economic stiflement of the colony prompted Brazilians a century later to propose sourly that books on Portuguese colonization of Brazil should be kept in the fiction section of the one public library which existed in the country. But at the time feelings ran deep, and resentment against what was now openly called exploitation erupted in 1789. Inspired by the American war of independence, a group of young men in Minas Gerais, led by José Joaquim da Silva Xavier, began the first organized movement for independence. Minas Gerais was the site of the gold mines which the Portuguese were feverishly working and the people of Minas knew exactly what exploitation meant. Silva Xavier had once been a dentist and he was known to his friends as *Tiradentes*, the 'Tooth-puller'. He was an idealist and deeply sincere and the plot which he and his young followers were hatching was nothing less than war against Portugal and the simultaneous proclamation of a republic on North American lines. The plotters had even designed Brazil's new flag for they were sure that once the revolt had been declared in Minas the rest of Brazil would rise too. They were still making their plans when the conspiracy was denounced by some of its own members. During his trial, Tiradentes tried to shoulder the entire responsibility for the plot, even refusing to give the names of any of his followers. In 1792 he alone was hanged by the Portuguese. Some of his closer followers were imprisoned, others were deported to Africa. The manner in which this plot was crushed was one of the rare instances of real brutality on the part of the Portuguese in the whole of Brazil's colonial history. Today, 'Tiradentes' stands in stone before what was the Chamber of Deputies in Rio before the transfer of the capital to Brasilia, a lone monument to the one martyr of Brazil's independence.

In 1807 Napoleon invaded Portugal and Dom João, the Prince Regent and Prince of Brazil, who was to become Dom João VI on the death of his mother, Queen Maria I, took refuge in Brazil with almost the entire Portuguese Court. On 29 November 1807, escorted by a British fleet, he sailed from the Tagus bound for Rio de Janeiro. The royal party consisted of more than 15,000 people and they travelled in sixty ships. It was a veritable mass migration of Portugal's aristocracy and of some of her richest merchants. A storm scattered the convoy and the eventual historic spectacle of the royal landing in Rio on 7 March 1808 is said to have been marred by one incident. Because of a virulent outbreak of lice during the ninety-nine days voyage from Lisbon, many of the Court ladies stepped ashore with their heads shaved. The gawking settlers dissolved in a gust of titters.

The transfer of the Court to Rio did much to quench the smouldering resentment against Portugal, although at first it had almost the opposite effect. Rio was hardly equipped to accommodate this sort of invasion and the appropriation by the Crown of the best houses in town for the use of noblemen and their families and servants aroused rumbles of protest even among the local Portuguese aristocracy. Brazilians became even more incensed by the contempt which members of the royal party showed for the primitive conditions of the capital. But it was the behaviour of Dom João's wife, Dona Carlota Joaquina, in particular which was even harder to bear. Frankly disgusted with the 'provincial', backward capital, her uninhibited comments were infinitely painful to the already touchy Brazilians. To peace-loving Dom João, his wife's intrigues and her often scandalous love affairs were profoundly distressing. Altogether, it was an inauspicious beginning to one of the most significant phases in Brazil's history.

Dom João was now able to see for himself what had been wrong for so long with his dominion. His first step was to end the policy of isolation. The Portuguese monopoly of trade was abolished and in the year of his arrival Brazilian ports were opened to foreign trade. During the thirteen years he remained in Brazil, Dom João tried to repair the damage done in the past by neglect and exploitation. He founded the Bank of Brazil, encouraged agriculture and cattle-raising, and in particular coffee and cotton-growing. Even the sugar industry in the north, which had virtually collapsed, because of the exodus from the coast to the gold and diamond fields, began to regain its former importance. He established medical and law schools and a military academy, founded industries and opened the gates wider to immigration; but it was still immigration from Portugal. His policies certainly strengthened the position of the growing economic aristocracy and the landed classes, but they did not change anybody else's life very much.

In 1814 Napoleon had been defeated and in 1815, by the deliberation of the Vienna Congress which had met to consider the problems left by the Napoleonic wars, Brazil was raised to the status of a kingdom. The Portuguese Empire was now known as the United Kingdom of Portugal, Brazil and the Algarves. But the decision was not well received in Lisbon. In 1816 Dom João had become

King on the death of his mother, Dona Maria I, and the Portuguese *Cortes* demanded his return. Dom João offered to send his son Pedro instead, for by now he was content to remain in Brazil and rule his Empire from Rio. In the end he realized that to do so would cost him his throne. While he still enjoyed a good deal of personal prestige in Brazil, the corruption and extravagance of his government was arousing bitter opposition. In 1817 a rebellion broke out in Pernambuco which was only put down with difficulty three months later.

Four years went by before Dom João bowed to the inevitable. On 22 April 1821 he named his son, Pedro, Regent, and two days later he sailed for Lisbon, leaving behind him for ever the country he had grown to love. But, sadly, he foresaw the future, and he left his son with these words: '. . . Should Brazil decide to separate herself from Portugal, let it be under your leadership rather than under one of these adventurers, since you are bound to respect me.' At the leave-taking, the discordant note was supplied as usual by Dona Carlota. It is said that she hung over the ship's side exultantly beating her slippers together to shake off the last particles of Brazilian dust.

4   The Frame of the Future. Independence

THE PORTUGUESE CORTES were not content merely with the return of Dom João. They proceeded to revoke many of the reforms he had introduced, for the Cortes were determined to restore Brazil to her colonial status. They also ordered Prince Pedro to return to Lisbon. From the very first, Pedro, as Regent, was in an intolerable situation. He was also torn by a conflict of conscience. He had not forgotten his father's words and in letters which he sometimes signed with his own blood he reaffirmed, time and again, his promise that he would never serve as an instrument for the separation of Brazil from the mother country.

Brazil was an autonomous kingdom, but the Portuguese, in their blind anxiety to regain their dominance, refused to recognize this fact. They challenged the existence of the government in Rio and insisted that each Brazilian province should organize its own assembly directly answerable to Lisbon; and the Cortes increased their pressure on the King to order the immediate return of his son to Europe. By their attitude they destroyed the feeling of allegiance to Portugal which, in fact, did exist in Brazil. Many Brazilians at the time accepted the possibility of the existence of two dominions of the House of Braganza, Portugal and Brazil, with their own sovereignty, but bound together by the bonds of common blood and heritage. Even Brazilian nationalist newspapers of the day spoke of the 'eternal links' which bound Brazil to Portugal.

But feelings in Brazil were beginning to run high. For Pedro, it was an agonizing dilemma. If he was to preserve the good which his father had done, and above all the unity and the identity of Brazil, which had been Dom João's greatest aim, he must disobey him; or, rather, disobey the edicts which the Cortes were imposing on his father. In his letters to Dom João, Pedro was now writing of the conflict in his mind.[3] Apart from personal considerations – after all, he was the heir to the throne of Portugal – he realized, too, that if he refused to return, as feelings now were in both Brazil and Portugal, it would be an inevitable step towards a complete separation. But refuse he did; and, on 7 September 1822, while on a visit to São Paulo, he received the latest peremptory dispatches from Lisbon. It was on the banks of Ypiranga, today a park in the city of São Paulo, that Pedro, in one of those theatrical gestures in which he liked to indulge, tore the Portuguese insignia from his tunic and, crying 'Independence or death!', broke his promise. Brazil's independence had been proclaimed.

Pedro was acclaimed King of Brazil. After all, the country had been a kingdom since 1815 and it was the natural title for him to assume and one which would be recognized by European courts. But nationalist feelings had been fanned into flame by the bigoted attitude of Lisbon which many Brazilians also regarded as a betrayal of their once sincere allegiance to Portugal and the House of Braganza. They wanted a title which would indicate an even more definite separation. The resentment at being so clumsily mishandled by Portugal persisted for a very long time. Their feelings had been dramatically summed up by Pedro on the banks of the Ypiranga: 'Comrades, Portugal wants to reduce Brazil to slavery'; and it is perhaps one reason why Brazilians today have remarkably little sentimental feeling for their mother country. There is no rancour left now, just indifference; almost derisive indifference. And so Pedro was declared the 'Constitutional Emperor of Brazil, Dom Pedro by the Grace of God and unanimous acclamation of the People'.

On 1 December 1822 he was not so much crowned as consecrated. By all accounts it was a remarkable ceremony. A French diplomat who attended seems to have been particularly struck with the Emperor's dress. He wore, so he reported, military uniform and large Russian cavalry boots. His crown and sceptre were traditional enough; but instead of an ermine pallium, he wore a cloak of birds' feathers in the manner of a *cacique*, an Indian chief. To the Brazilians, however, this garb was felicitously appropriate. To them, it was symbolic of the spirit of the new Empire, a blend of the traditional, the liberal revolutionary and of the native American Indian. It was a happy, Sunday-like atmosphere; for, in a surge of pride and rejoicing, the Brazilians were sure that now, under Pedro, Brazil would flourish as a New World Empire – an American empire.[4]

The first problem which faced Pedro was the recognition of Brazil's independence by Portugal. Portugal was once again under an absolutist régime and the countries of the Holy Alliance, fearing the recognition of the Empire of Brazil would mean serious loss of prestige for legitimatist principles, advised war. It was largely thanks to England that such a war was prevented. After fruitless negotiations between Brazil and Portugal, Canning warned the Portuguese government that Britain, despite her old alliance, would not support Portugal in her refusal to accord recognition. Nor would she help her in facing the likely disastrous consequences of this attitude. In the end, it was an Englishman, Sir Charles Stuart, whom the Portuguese agreed to accept as a mediator, who helped to bring about recognition. One stipulation was that the two Crowns should remain within the House of Braganza. But Britain insisted that Brazil should accept one important condition in return for her support. This was the abolition of slavery and it was something little short of an economic revolution which the new Empire was being asked to accept; and this condition was to arouse a great deal of resentment years later, during the Second Empire.

A Treaty of Recognition was finally signed on 29 August 1825, and it provoked such violent opposition in Portugal that it might never have been ratified. Britain, however, reiterated her stand that, as she was prepared to recognize the new Spanish-American Republics, she would not make an exception in the case of Brazil. George Canning, in 1826, summed up Britain's interest in the welfare of these new republics when he said: 'I have called the New World into existence to redress the balance of the old.' Britain's motives were not entirely altruistic, there were trade and other considerations, but she did play a decisive role in bringing about the emergence of many of these new states, just as later British capital helped to lay the foundations of their economies.

South American historians recall, often gratefully, Britain's role in their affairs, but the people of these countries today have only a vague idea of what this role was. It is the same in Brazil. Nevertheless, of all the foreigners who went to Brazil, the British are among the few who still enjoy a very great measure of esteem and respect. In the conduct of their business and in their behaviour generally, the British built up a store of goodwill and it still exists. Few people in Britain today seem to realize this. More remarkable still is the fact that although many Brazilians now may have only a hazy idea of what Britain's role has been in their history, few Englishmen seem to have any idea at all that their country even played such a role in this New World.

With recognition from Portugal achieved at last, Brazilians now felt that their sovereignty had been truly consummated. But there was still friction, not only between the two countries but in Brazil itself between the Brazilians and those settlers who still considered themselves to be wholly Portuguese. Although the popularity of the Emperor was by no means as great as it had been less than three years before, and his government was arousing rumbles of protest, on the whole the Brazilians still glowed with high hopes for the future. Certainly, Brazil was no longer isolated nor was she quite the intel- lectual desert which Dom João had found seventeen years earlier. Yet much of the atmosphere of a colony still existed. When it is said that 'Brazilians' still glowed with hope, these Brazilians were those who lived in, and virtually owned, the developed areas of the country; and those areas then were very few indeed. In the early days of the Empire, Brazil's population was probably around four million. Negro slaves accounted for about half of this, for slavery still flourished, and it was only thirty-three years later, in 1855, that the slave trade was prohibited. In 1871 a law provided for a gradual emancipation of slaves, but it was only in 1888 that slavery was abolished entirely.

The fundamental pattern of society was based on agriculture and it was essentially a feudal society. The seeds of Brazil's poverty today were planted a long time ago. And yet, in the early nineteenth century, although the class structure was rigid, it was not exactly a caste system. It was virtually impossible for a man to ascend the social ladder, but there was a measure of contact between the strata. On the whole, even the slaves were not maltreated and the Brazilian aristocracy, at least at that time, exercised a far greater degree of tolerance and charity than the descendants of the Spanish rulers ever did in other parts of the continent. Tolerance is still one of the most heart-warming characteristics of the Brazilian today, yet ironically this tolerance also bred a philosophical acceptance of the unfairness inherent in such a social structure, and the remarkable thing is that it should have lasted for so long. Even today the great mass of Brazilians, including the Negro who is experiencing a subtle, almost tacit discrimination, still tend to accept inequalities almost as a matter of predestination. It is only very recently that some of these inhabitants of this other world of Brazil, the world of the have-nots, have begun to revolt. But here again, as we shall see, their revolt has taken some unique and peculiarly Brazilian twists.

Despite the great expectations, independence and the advent of the Empire did not make any great difference to the everyday life of ordinary Brazilians; except, perhaps, for the Negro slaves. They eventually gained their freedom, although even that, for them, turned out to be a mixed blessing. Yet it was during the Empire, a period of experiment which lasted for sixty-seven years, that Brazil acquired a great many of her characteristic political and social traits. Pedro's reign lasted exactly eight years and four months. His guide and counsellor even before independence had been a Brazilian, José Bonifacio de Andrada e Silva, who became his Minister of the Interior and Foreign Affairs. He was one of the first Brazilian statesmen and perhaps the ablest man of his time.

José Bonifacio deserves to be remembered because in many ways he was the precursor of the elder statesmen, although often they have not been politicians, who have always come forward in Brazil's worst crises to help to avert what seemed to be inevitable disaster. Such men have not worked miracles on their own, often they have been simply rallying figures for the forces of reason, which have also been ready and waiting in the wings. José Bonifacio was born in Brazil in 1763. He became a professor of geology in Portugal at the University of Coimbra and later Inspector General of Portuguese mines. He was elected perpetual Secretary of the Lisbon Academy. He returned to Brazil in 1819 and it was he who guided Pedro in his anguished decision not to return to Portugal. He was also, perhaps, the principal architect of Brazil's independence. If only Pedro had listened to him more often and more carefully in latter years, his reign and perhaps even the fate of the Empire might have been different.

Counselling the Emperor was no easy matter. Pedro had a great many qualities and at first the interests of Brazil were undoubtedly his main concern. But he was impetuous and often extremely temperamental and at heart he was an authoritarian. His nature was simply not attuned to the restrictions of a constitutional monarchy such as men like José Bonifacio hoped for. The Constituent Assembly which he called shortly after he was crowned was acclaimed by Brazilians as their first representative parliament, although very few of them had much say in the choice of their representatives. But within this Assembly there were so many divergences of opinion, so many clashes of personality, that Pedro found it unmanageable. In November 1823 he dissolved it. He had become thoroughly impatient, too, with his old counsellor, José Bonifacio, together with his liberal ideas. He dismissed him and when the Assembly was dissolved banished him from Brazil. For six years José Bonifacio remained in exile in France.

Brazilians were getting their first taste of political turmoil and it was to be something which during the generations that followed they were to become only too familiar with. Yet, however bitter these political conflicts became at times, and despite risings in the provinces, they never exploded into mass violence. Some form of conciliation was usually reached even though it might not have lasted for very long. These triumphs of reason over force have been a characteristic of Brazil's political history ever since. Even Pedro was made to realize in the end that he was going too far. The Constitution which he introduced in March 1824 gave some expression to the liberal feelings which existed at the time. Although the

Crown still retained the role of moderator, the Constitution now provided for an elected Lower House and a Senate to be elected by the Crown. Ministers and a Council of State would be appointed by the Emperor, who also had the power to dissolve the Chamber of Deputies and to suspend any acts of the legislature. It also guaranteed a certain measure of religious freedom, the equality of citizens in the eyes of the law, at least in principle, and freedom of speech and of the press. The Brazilian press has been remarkably free ever since. It has never been restricted either systematically or for any long period except during the Vargas dictatorship of the 1930s. This Constitution remained in force throughout the remaining days of the Empire, a period of sixty-five years.

With the new Constitution, Pedro was able, for a time, to pacify some of his more vociferous political critics. But he had other faults. Brazilians today read about his romantic adventures and particularly of his affair with the Marquesa de Santos with amusement and a feeling of warm affection. The years have created an image of him as a romantic and very human sort of person. But at the time, Brazilians were not amused. His behaviour was often scandalous, in fact, in many ways he was very much his mother's son, Dona Carlota Joaquina whom Brazilians still recalled with a wince. There was also a great deal of sympathy for his wife, the Empress, Dona Leopoldina, a Hapsburg and the daughter of the Emperor of Austria; a gentle, kindly woman whom poorer Brazilians had come to call the 'mother of the needy'. There was resentment, too, of the influence which the Marquesa de Santos exercised over the Emperor and the feeling also got around that Pedro was finding the everyday business of government tedious. Worse still, Brazilians began to feel that their Emperor was not really a Brazilian, which of course was true. Pedro may have defied the Cortes when he proclaimed Brazil's independence, that was an expression of the rebellious streak in his character, but in his heart he was always very much a Portuguese.

One of the most disastrous events of his reign was the war with Argentina over the present-day tiny republic of Uruguay on the northern banks of the Plate estuary. It had been part of Spanish America, but the Portuguese wanted to take the borders of Brazil down to the Plate, arguing that the estuary was a natural frontier between the Spanish and Portuguese domains. This wedge of land had become a growing source of friction between the two countries. While Dom João VI was in Brazil it was taken and garrisoned by Portuguese troops but later a treaty was negotiated which, in fact, extended Brazil's borders down to the Plate. This disputed territory became the Brazilian province of Cisplatina. But the Uruguayans had no wish to belong either to Spain or Portugal. When Brazil proclaimed her independence they began to fight even harder for their own sovereignty. Uruguay appealed to Argentina for help and Brazilians suddenly found themselves involved in a war with their largest neighbours. It seemed all the more futile because many Brazilians frankly sympathized with the Uruguayans and they felt almost a sense of shame at being entangled in this kind of war. Britain finally intervened and peace was brought about between the two countries. In 1828 Uruguay became independent; but the costly war with Argentina had a great deal to do with Pedro's growing unpopularity.

For some time now, Pedro was being distracted by another problem which had nothing to do with Brazil. In Portugal, his daughter, Queen Maria II, was being challenged by her uncle, Dom Miguel, Pedro's younger brother, who was seeking to seize the throne. Harassed by his constant quarrels with parliament and his ministers and with the army turned against him, but worried even more, so it would seem, by what was happening in Portugal, Pedro, in a last dramatic gesture, decided to abdicate in favour of his son, Pedro d'Alcantara, who was then barely five years old. To be his son's guardian, he named the man who had become his greatest critic and opponent in parliament: José Bonifacio, who had been allowed to return to Brazil in 1829. On 7 April 1831 Pedro sailed for Lisbon.[5]

After all that had happened, one might have expected the Brazilians to feel thoroughly disillusioned with the Empire. They were bitterly disappointed with Pedro but it was not the end of the Empire. A ten-year Regency period followed, during which the Brazilians' capacity for tolerance, improvisation and reason was strained to the limit. The Constitution of 1824 laid down that in the event of the heir to the throne being a minor the country would be ruled by a three-man Regency until he reached the age of eighteen. It was the choice of these regents which gave rise to the first real political struggles. Members of the Assembly had little experience of parliamentary rules and procedure and in their frenzy to put forward their ideas, sessions of the Assembly were often transformed into almost pure *opéra bouffe*. Rival factions fought fiercely for the nomination of their own candidates for the Regency. Yet, out of this pandemonium, some form of parliamentary organization was born. The various currents of such public opinion as there was crystallized into parties. The two main ones were the Moderates, who upheld the Regency, and the Restorists, who wanted the return of Pedro I. During this time, the Brazilian politician was born. To the man in the street, however, he was a remote figure, carrying on polemics about which he often could not feel very strongly nor even understand. To these Brazilians, parliament seemed to be something quite apart from their everyday life; and it is a feeling which persists to some extent even today.

Dom Pedro died in Portugal five years after his abdication and the Restoration Party died with him. Much of the tumult in parliament had been caused by the existence of these Restorists who were so often accused, in angry, rowdy debates, of being what today would be called the tools of Portuguese imperialism, the saboteurs of nationalism. The political forces in the country now grouped themselves into two broad categories, the conservatives and the liberals, and it marked the point when Brazil became finally free of the last remnants of political influence from Portugal. During this noisy, often chaotic Regency period, the Assembly nevertheless did find time to put through some important legislation. It promulgated a penal code and decreed a constitutional amendment which gave more autonomy to the provincial legislative assemblies. It also decreed the first penalties for slave importers, but this was purely theoretical legislation.

Throughout the Regency period, two Triumvirates and later two successive Regents tried to cope with the growing feeling of unrest in the provinces, particularly in the far south, and with the insubordination and lawlessness in the army. In this darkening atmosphere of political and personal rivalries Brazilians began to feel in despair that the only solution was the rallying influence of the throne. Pedro I was dead; but there was his son, Pedro d'Alcantara, in whom, although he was still a boy, the advocaters of this solution hopefully noted outstanding traits of character and intelligence. These Brazilians reminded each other that young Pedro was much more like his mother, the quiet, levelheaded Empress Leopoldina, than his unpredictable, autocratic father. And so, on 23 July 1840, he was declared of age. He was not quite fifteen years old. On 18 July of the following year he was crowned Pedro II.

5   The Empire and the other Pedro

WITH THE ADVENT OF THE SECOND EMPEROR the glow of hope for the future returned, although it was not quite as warm as it had been when Pedro I had come to the throne. Brazilians had experienced barely twenty years of independence, but during that time they had suffered a war which had lasted for five years. They had watched governments and regencies disintegrate in clouds of recrimination and lost battles as their new leaders, or at least some of them, fought bravely but vainly to bring unity and a new sense of purpose to a land which was already split before independence. Regional rivalries, and to some extent ethnical differences, but above all resentment of the powers of the Central government, were fanning feelings of revolt in the provinces. There was already a republican movement, but it was to be a long time yet before these republicans were able to make their voice heard. On the whole, Brazilians still pinned their hopes on the Empire and on the unifying influence of the Crown.

But what ordinary Brazilians still could not realize was any real feeling of concern for their own welfare; and they had to wait a long time before they did begin to realize it, for Brazil, for many years to come, was to be a land of opportunity only for an educated, privileged minority. Brazilians were already beginning to suspect politicians as a body. The politicians themselves had not shown any great trust in each other either. The Crown, it was felt, would at least be above purely political considerations and personal ambitions. This mistrust of politicians *en masse* has persisted; even in present-day elections the ordinary Brazilian tends to place more trust in the individual rather than in parties. Given the chance, he would vote for an independent, and we shall see how these feelings have grown and with what results, when we look at Brazil's recent history.

Pedro II came to the throne of a country whose morale had become badly shaken, but even more so by the Regency period than by the stormy reign of the first Emperor. More than ever, Brazilians of the north and the far south regarded Rio as remote and aloof from their problems and aspirations. These smouldering resentments erupted in rebellions in Maranhão, São Paulo, Minas Gerais and Rio Grande do Sul. It was inevitable, in a country so large and where communications were almost non-existent, that this feeling of separation between different regions should develop. The remark-able thing is that Brazil should have remained united as a country, for this sense of spiritual isolation and of local identity grew. Even as late as the early 1930s there was a movement in the state of São Paulo, already by far the most prosperous region in the country and with an identity of its own, to break away from the rest of Brazil. The Paulistas claimed that their energy and enterprise were being exploited. What many of them felt was summed up in the slogan of the separatist movement, that São Paulo was the locomotive which drew the empty wagons of the other Brazilian states. The army, too, was almost as divided in its loyalties; and the hoped-for solution to all these problems, the rallying point and the unifying force which was to give Brazilians a renewed sense of purpose, was a boy barely sixteen years old.

Dom Pedro II was almost the complete antithesis of his father.[6] His had been a lonely and a sad childhood. He had been brought up in the isolated atmosphere of the court, with little contact with the world beyond the palace gardens and none at all with the other members of the Royal House to which he belonged. Even as he grew older, he always seemed oppressed by the role which had been thrust upon him. He was a quiet, scholarly, essentially serious youth. His interests were in his books and in the arts; he once admitted that his ambition was to be a schoolmaster. Nevertheless, he took very seriously the task of government, a pursuit which had bored his father and whose only known excursion into the arts had been to tease his mistress by painting delicately traced insects on her bedroom walls.

An extremely good-looking man in his youth, Pedro, as he grew older, developed an impressive and dignified presence. He was also genuinely modest. He never went out of his way to publicize his acts, although many of them were to have a lasting and invaluable effect on the course of Brazil's history. Dedicated as he was in his personal conduct to the cause of the Empire, he made no real effort to maintain this régime when it was finally and truly challenged. On occasions he even expressed admiration for the republican form of government; and in a strange document written by him and published after his death there are many and precise considerations of his country's political and other problems, but no suggestion as to the best form of government to solve them, and no reference at all to the dynasty. His unconventional attitudes, which often shocked conventional royalists in Europe, endeared him to the people of North America. There was even a bizarre movement to put forward his name as a candidate for president of the United States.

When he came to the throne he was, inevitably, surrounded by a host of advisers; but he was fortunate, although perhaps it was due to some instinctive wisdom in one so young, that he was well advised. Throughout his reign, one of his marked characteristics was to distinguish between good and bad advice, although later he was to pay even closer attention to the dictates of his own conscience. In a very short time Pedro II was making his own decisions. Chroniclers of the time noted that even as a youth he seemed intent on observing the behaviour of men around him, studying the ways in which their prejudices could cloud their judgment. To many of his courtiers and advisers it was often a disconcerting experience. He also had an insatiable curiosity, but it was essentially an intellectual curiosity. The material world of politics must have offended his nature; but he rarely showed it. His reign lasted for forty-eight years and it is sometimes argued that the Empire might have lasted much longer if only he had taken more account of the political implications of some of his reforms. Nevertheless, these forty-eight years were one of the most significant and constructive periods in Brazil's history. For one thing, Pedro succeeded in performing something which was little short of a miracle; he restored dignity and authority to parliament. Although, under the constitution of 1824, he had very considerable powers, he exercised his prerogatives with a sense of responsibility and a concern for the country's interests which were remarkable for the times. Later, his critics were to accuse him of sacrificing those interests to moral principles in one notable instance. That was during the campaign for the abolition of slavery. Nevertheless, the high moral standards he set the administration were such that officials often left office poorer than when they entered it; and that, too, was something of a revolution.

It was during his reign that Brazil experienced its first real surge of progress, with the building of railways; the construction of ship-yards; the opening up of roads and the encouragement of foreign capital. At the close of his reign the value of Brazil's trade was almost five times greater than it was when he came to the throne. By the end of 1888 over 130,000 immigrants had also come into the country through the ports of Rio de Janeiro and Santos, although much of this immigration was due more to the initiative of the provincial government of São Paulo; and it was these immigrants who helped to build the foundations of the great commercial and industrial centre which São Paulo is today. Around the middle of the century, Canadians founded the Light and Power Company which was to construct in São Paulo and Rio some of the largest power plants in all Latin America and they paved the way for Brazil's modern industrialization. In the 1860s, the British began to build the São Paulo railway, and it is still one of the notable engineering feats of the world. The railway gave the growing city of São Paulo and the surrounding farming and coffee-producing country their outlet to the sea. Tunnelling and winding its way down the 2,600-foot escarp-ment of the Serra do Mar to the coast, it transformed Santos into the coffee port of the world. During Pedro's reign the first submarine cable was laid linking Brazil to Europe. In 1851 the first population census of the country was carried out. This showed that Brazil had a population of just over seven million. Thirty-eight years later, in 1889, the year in which the Empire fell, the population had risen to almost 14 million.

Brazil was beginning to achieve recognition in the world and a great deal of this was due to the respect which Pedro II aroused on his excursions abroad. He went to Europe three times, travelling in England, France and Italy. In 1876 he visited the United States. These visits did much to stoke up interest in Brazil, a country which to many Europeans, and even Americans, was still very much of a mystery. But back at home, in the provinces, the dangerous mood of rebellion persisted. To some extent the Emperor succeeded in bringing about a kind of peace throughout the country; but not without the bloodshed which his nature revolted against. He entrusted the campaign of pacifying the provinces, which Brazilians of the capital had come to refer to as the 'interior', to a young colonel who was later to rise to the rank of marshal with the title of Duke of Caxias. It was Caxias who reorganized the divided and often disorderly Brazilian army and transformed it into a force which was to play a decisive role in Brazil's political scene ever afterwards. While José Bonifacio became the patriarch of Brazil's independence, Caxias became the architect of her defences.

Another problem which Brazil faced at this time, and it took thirty years and a great many lives before it was finally settled, were the conflicts and frontier disputes with her southern neighbours. In the latter days of Spanish rule the South American colonies had been apportioned into four Vice-Royalties; one of these was La Plata, which consisted of a territory now divided into the republics of Argentina, Uruguay, Paraguay and Bolivia. But trouble between different factions among the colonists of this territory continued even after it had split up into independent states, and there was a constant movement of troops along Brazil's southerly borders. These troops frequently invaded Brazilian territory in search of supplies, sacking and plundering settlements as far south as Rio Grande. Unlike the war which Pedro I had waged against Argentina, on this occasion national pride was involved. Brazil again declared war on Argentina; and later, in 1865, she joined forces with Argentina and Uruguay to fight against the expansionist ambitions of Solano López who had set himself up not only as dictator of Paraguay at the head of a remarkably powerful military machine for its times; but also he aspired to be the Napoleon of South America. The conquest of a part of southwestern Brazil was one of his dreams.

The campaign directed by Caxias against Paraguay lasted for five years, and towards the end it was waged almost entirely by Brazil, for the Argentine and Uruguayan troops were constantly being recalled to put down revolts in their own countries. In its own way, it was one of the most tragic wars in history. The Paraguayans fought with fanatical bravery; every able-bodied Paraguayan was put into the field, and that included women and even children of twelve. At the beginning of the war, Paraguay had a population of just over 1,338,000. On her defeat, five years later, her surviving people were estimated to be fewer than 250,000, of whom only about 29,000 were male. But, characteristically, Brazil did not annex Paraguay, nor did she take any further punitive measures. Solano López was dead and Brazil set about helping to repair some of the ravages of the war. To this day, Brazilians have a special feeling of warmth for the Paraguayans. Although Brazil did intervene in the internal affairs of these countries of the former Vice-Royalty of La Plata, it was, as history shows, to defend her frontiers, not extend them. This policy of non-interference with others has been one of the basic principles of Brazil's foreign policy ever since. It was essentially this policy which prompted her, a century later, to resist for so long the growing pressure from Washington to break off relations with Cuba, despite the fact that economically she had become increasingly dependent on American goodwill. She only broke with Cuba in 1964, after the overthrow of the left-wing government of President João Goulart; and she only did so when the right-wing caretaker government felt that there was evidence of Cuban meddling in Brazilian affairs. But a great many Brazilians were not happy even about this; to them, not to intervene in other people's business, however indirectly, is more than just a matter of official policy; it has become a sacred principle.

During the Second Empire, Brazil was evolving not only materially but mentally. Brazilians were acquiring a sense of national identity; but it was not a nationalist conscience, although the issue of slavery and the test of the Paraguayan war had shown that

Brazilians could be united. The great gaps in the thinking, but, above all, in social levels and in the conditions of life in different regions had not been bridged. Brazil was beginning to separate even more distinctly into three worlds: the growing and prosperous world of the south, and that of the already struggling north. Behind these was that vast, green darkness, the almost deserted world of the interior. The Brazilians of that time were also a very different people. They were still either transplanted Portuguese or the product of miscegenation. The stream of immigrants had not yet begun and when it did it was to make some of the contrasts in Brazil, particularly between the north and the south, all the sharper. It also created another and very different type of Brazilian.

Culturally, Brazil had not advanced much either, despite the Emperor's essentially intellectual temperament. This is not surprising when one remembers that for three centuries after her discovery almost any form of cultural development was methodically suppressed. Before 1800, even the publication of newspapers was forbidden. Throughout her colonial days and to some extent even after independence, such education as existed was the prerogative of the Church and the religious orders. Attempts were made to enlarge the work and the scope of the cultural institutions which Dom João VI had founded during his sojourn in Brazil, and there were stirrings of cultural development in sculpture, architecture and literature. But cultural enlightenment was still at the candlelight stage. At the end of Pedro II's reign, 90 per cent of the population was wholly illiterate; and the great majority of Brazilians were to remain illiterate for a very long time; long after illiteracy elsewhere was no longer considered by the ruling classes to be the natural state of the lower orders.

Against this background of primitive backwardness, the sophistication and even the degree of culture of the minority, the economic aristocracy and their representatives, in what often seemed to be the ivory tower of parliament, is all the more striking. But during the Second Empire, parliament had acquired a new dignity and evolved a character and an orderliness which were unique in South America. Parliamentary business was now conducted almost with elegance, and members had their eyes constantly turned on the customs and political procedure of European countries, but in particular England. Although the Brazilian intellectual had a more natural inclination towards French culture, the greatest praise that could be bestowed on a Brazilian politician was to say that he belonged to the classic English school. Members meticulously adopted the English way of dress, even to the top hat and frock coat which they wore heroically in all seasons; and in the Rio summer it must have been torture indeed. The desire to follow Westminster's example was such that, as one can see from the records of the time, there was hardly ever a major debate in which members did not quote from British parlia/mentary debates. These records abound with references to English precedents and quotations from the speeches of Peel and Palmerston and Gladstone. London was the Mecca to which almost every political figure of the time aspired to make his pilgrimage, and many of them did. The London *Times* was almost required reading. The second Emperor himself was a devout admirer of Queen Victoria, whom he regarded as a model of the constitutional monarch. With the advent of the Republic, the character of the Brazilian parliament changed too. But it was some time before this influence and the inspiration of Westminster faded, although it never faded entirely.

During the Second Empire trade steadily increased, but Brazil's economy and the life of the country were still based on agriculture. There was virtually no industry; according to an 1850 census there were only fifty factories in the whole country, and many of these must have been little more than cottage industries. There was very little incentive for the Brazilians to start industries. For one thing, there were no tariffs to protect them and no real domestic market to encourage them. Under a treaty signed between Britain and Dom João VI, tariffs on British goods had been substantially reduced and in time other manufacturing countries pressed for, and secured similar treatment. But the Brazilians themselves, that is the rich Brazilians – the rest of the population hardly counted as consumers – demanded foreign goods, not only because of their quality but as a matter of prestige. This prejudice against the locally manufactured article persisted long after Brazilian industry had begun to match the quality of many imported goods. Even up to the beginning of the Second World War many a society hostess would not dream of offending her guests by expecting them to eat off anything so vulgar as a Brazilian-made plate.

During his long reign Pedro II had brought about a revolution. There was a new spirit in Brazil and an exhilarating feeling of belonging to the world. The fact that his régime lasted for almost forty-eight uninterrupted years was in itself something unique in the New World. But the Brazilian Empire had lasted for sixty-seven years. The nineteenth century was a time of revolt and great up-heavals in the world. France, which intellectual Brazilians regarded as the fountain-head of culture, experienced ten changes of govern-ment in the course of a century. Even the United States, as Brazilian historians also like to point out, had not been able to achieve the abolition of slavery without one of the bloodiest civil wars the world has ever known. The Brazilian Empire had not been exactly an era of peace and prosperity and the advent of the Republic was to be the beginning of another period of conflict and unrest even greater than Brazil had experienced during the days of the Regency. But Brazil-ians did feel that they had achieved a great deal, and without anything like the squandering of blood which had happened else-where. A tribute to Pedro II paid by Rui Barbosa, one of the great statesmen of the new Republic, reflected what Brazilians still feel about him and his reign; and yet in a sense they also feel it was more of a tribute to themselves. Rui Barbosa notes that during Pedro's reign Brazil advanced enormously, but he goes on to ask: was it because of the Emperor? According to this staunch republican, it was not; it was due more to the spontaneous development of the spirit of nationality in the Brazilian; although he concedes that without a doubt this spirit developed under the influence and with the co-operation of the Emperor. The praise is not as grudging as it sounds. Rui Barbosa, like many another statesman of the Republic, had a great deal of admiration for Pedro's personal qualities, if not for his political acumen. It was this disregard of political consequences which in the end destroyed him and the Empire.

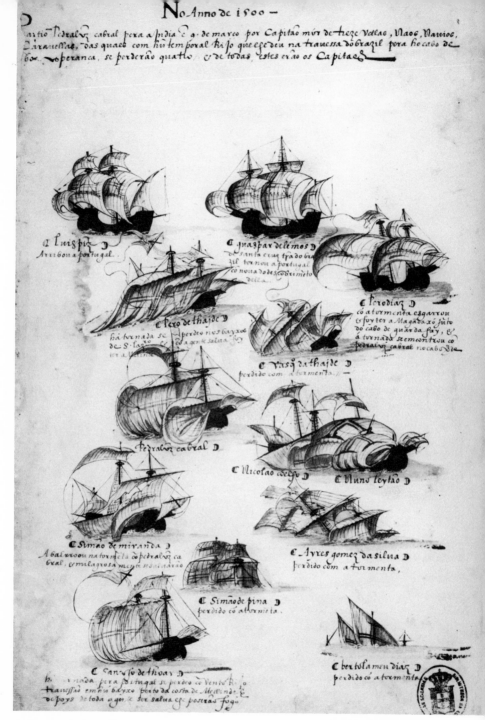

16 In 1500 Pedro Albares Cabral, a Portuguese admiral on a voyage to India, discovered Brazil by chance. This sixteenth-century print shows Cabral's fleet.

17 Portugal's claim to Brazil was being challenged by the time this map was made in 1593, especially by France and Holland.

18 Potential German colonizers received a far from friendly reception from the natives. A sixteenth-century print.

19 The Portuguese attempted administration by dividing Brazil into fiefs, or *capitanias*. São Vicente (later São Paulo) was a principal one. A sixteenth-century print.

20 A central government for all Brazil was established in Rio de Janeiro in 1763. This plan of Rio dates from 1555 when the French colonizer Nicholas de Villegaignon occupied Rio Harbour.

21 The Dutch invaded Brazil in 1624 and Brazilian captives were taken to Holland as seen in this seventeenth-century print.

S. Salvador

22 Manuel da Nóbrega, one of the many Jesuit missionaries who came to Brazil in the sixteenth century. A 1938 sculpture by Franciscus Franco.

23 Jesuits laid the foundations of education and the Christian faith among the Indians. A somewhat fanciful nineteenth-century representation of the first Mass in Brazil by Vítor Meirelles.

24 Except for a period of sixty years of Spanish rule, Brazil remained a Portuguese colony until 1822. This is the ceremony of recognition of the Portuguese king, Dom João VI in 1816.

25 In 1821, at the insistence of the Portuguese Cortes, João VI returned to Portugal. The departure of his Queen, Dona Carlotta Joaquina. Both engravings of the nineteenth century by J. B. Debret.

26 Dom João left his son as Regent, who later became Pedro I, first Emperor of Brazil. A scene on the day of his coronation from an engraving of the nineteenth century by J. B. Debret.

27 José Bonifacio de Andrada e Silva (1763–1838) was the father of Brazil's independence and one of the first Brazilian statesmen.

28 In 1831 Pedro I abdicated, leaving his son as Regent. In 1840 he was crowned Pedro II.

29 The reign of Pedro II was an era of progress. The São Paulo railway, built by the British in the 1860s, is one of the great engineering feats of the world.

6   The Crumbling Foundations

IN THE LATTER YEARS OF HIS REIGN Pedro II lost in turn the support of the three great powers which had been the pillars of the Empire: the Church, the landowners and the army. Although the antagonism of the landowners was the most bitter, and in the end it was the army which played the decisive role in the destruction of the Empire, the resentment of the Church and of militant Catholic opinion grew perhaps the more insidious roots.

The Imperial Constitution of 1824 laid down that the official religion would be the Roman Catholic faith, and the whole system of relations between Church and State which existed in Portugal now also existed in Brazil. It was a relationship which had led to frequent conflicts between the civil power and the Church, particularly during Pombal's government in Portugal. The Church in Brazil was not a rich institution. It remained almost entirely a charge on the State which, ever since colonial days, had received the income from ecclesiastical taxes. In 1854 the entry of novices into religious orders had been suspended, and since then the situation of the Church had steadily deteriorated. The great monasteries and convents, inhabited now mostly by the elderly, had lost much of their influence. The bishops, on the other hand, fared very much better; they were directly appointed by the Crown. Pedro II was by temperament a liberal and, although respectful and devout, he was not an unquestioning upholder of ecclesiastical authority. It was an attitude which not only disturbed the traditionalists; it was to be exploited later in the republican cause.

Ever since independence, freemasonry had been spreading in Brazil. It had been a link between the various separatist organizations, an underground force in the movement for independence. It was a political and patriotic society and apparently aloof from the philosophical and religious contentions which were sweeping Europe. As such, it had attracted many prominent people including priests and members of the religious orders. But the situation was to change as interest in the role of European freemasonry grew. Echoes of the Italians struggle for unification, of the 1848 revolution and the Roman Question had reached Brazil and Brazilian newspapers had begun to attack ecclesiastical institutions. The old prelates, who had grown impassive in almost any situation which arose, remained silent. Two prominent figures of the clergy, however, did not. They were the Bishops of Recife and Pará, who reacted by ordering the expulsion of freemasons from the religious brotherhoods and orders. When these protested, the bishops closed the churches to them. Instead of taking their case to the supreme religious authorities, they appealed to the Crown. The Council of State ruled that the bishops, as state-appointed functionaries, had exceeded their rights, since the papal authority on which they had based their decisions had not been approved by the civil power. The bishops retorted that they had acted exclusively within their spiritual jurisdiction. The conflict had begun.

The bishops refused to revoke their interdict. The Cabinet, which at the time was headed by Viscount Rio Branco, who incidentally was Grand Master of Brazilian masonry, proceeded against them as recalcitrant public servants. As such, the bishops were found guilty, although later there was an amnesty and the issue was dropped. But the Holy See, which initially had remained discreetly silent over this issue, had come forward unequivocally in defence of the bishops when their authority was legally challenged. The result of all this was a deep feeling of unrest and a great many troubled consciences. Although the Church did not openly switch its support to the republican cause, as the landowners were to do later, the alliance which had existed between Church and Crown was destroyed.

The other, and infinitely more serious, crisis was over the issue of slavery. The wealth of Brazil and her whole economy were based on agriculture and mining and both depended entirely on slave labour. Any meddling with the institution of slavery was obviously highly dangerous. The landowners were the richest and the most influential class in the land, and even today, although industrialization has created a new *élite*, they are still the basis of the Brazilian establish, ment. It was from this aristocracy that the nation's representatives in parliament were chosen. The Brazilians' attitude to slavery had long been very different from what it was, for example, in North America. Without ignoring the moral issues involved, they tended to regard it also as a practical problem. No theorists ever propounded the ethni, cal inferiority of the Negro, nor were there any extreme defenders of the institution of slavery as such. Everyone, even the *élite*, felt that slavery must end. The problem was, when should it end, and, above all, how could it be ended. Immigration was the obvious solution, but there was very little incentive for an immigrant to settle in Brazil. The chances of his becoming even a small landowner were virtually non,existent.

One might come to the cynical conclusion that the Brazilians were merely trying to square their conscience over this whole issue while doing very little else about it. The latter was certainly true, but slavery was to weigh very heavily on their conscience as the years went by. One must also remember that, from the very beginning of slavery, to the Portuguese settlers and later to the Brazilians, the Negroes, particularly the women, meant very much more than just units of labour, and Brazilians felt that their slaves were, on the whole, at least well treated; which was also true. In fact, relations between master and slave often became laced with a good deal of affection and even respect.

In 1850, barely ten years after Pedro II had come to the throne, it was calculated that there were some four million slaves in Brazil. Slaves, in fact, accounted for over half of the known population of the entire country. In 1864, the year before slavery was abolished in the United States, the number of slaves had dropped to about two million, while the population had grown to almost nine million. But long before 1850 public opinion in Europe, particularly in England, had been outraged by the continuation of this 'barbarous' state of affairs in Brazil which had shocked Darwin during his voyage round South America in the early 1830s. It was recalled that

Brazil, as far back as 1825, had solemnly pledged herself to abolish slavery in return for England's support in her efforts to secure Portgual's recognition of her independence. In 1830 a law had been passed outlawing the slave trade, but for twenty years it was to be a purely theoretical step. Brazilians reaction to this anti-slavery crusade, this condemnation by Europe and particularly England, was characteristic.

Brazilians considered themselves to be very much a part of Western civilization and they were undoubtedly ashamed at being branded as barbaric. But an even deeper emotion was one of bitter resentment at the apparent lack of understanding of their problem. When the Aberdeen Act was passed in 1845, which asserted the right of the British navy to intercept slave ships in Brazilian waters, the Brazilians almost exploded. There was even a rumbling move-ment to declare war on England and many Brazilians who once condemned slavery, Brazilians who were not landowners and who had no interest in the slave trade, executed a smart volte-face. The institution of slavery was no longer regarded only in the light of a moral issue and a disgrace to the country; national pride was also involved now. Many Brazilians still agreed that slavery was a bad thing and a problem which must be solved, but it was their problem and one which they would solve themselves in their own way and in their own time; and damnation to treaties and foreign interference. The Aberdeen Bill was openly challenged, but not just out of bravado. The landowners, the mine-owners and the slave traders realized that the days of imported slave labour were numbered, and so in the five years after the passing of the Bill the import of slaves increased sharply; according to some accounts it trebled. It is esti-mated that slaves were being brought in at the rate of almost sixty thousand a year. But despite the resentment against the effrontery of foreigners who presumed to dictate to the Brazilians what they should do about slavery, there was still a strong abolitionist movement in the country and in the government.

As public opinion became less inflamed the abolitionist move-ment grew; and the dominant figure in this movement was the Emperor, constantly prodding it to move faster. The abolitionists faced formidable opposition, and not only in parliament. Slaves were very big business and there was the well-organized slave trade, mostly in the hands of Portuguese, to fight, to say nothing of the landowners who wielded tremendous influence. The resistance of the slave traders and landowners to attempts to enforce any embargo on the slave trade at times exploded into violence, but they were isolated incidents and in 1854 the government did succeed in outlawing the slave trade. As far as is known, 1855 saw the arrival of the last slave ship from Africa. But there was still the problem of the slaves born in Brazil; these, particularly the women, now became an even more precious commodity. In the past, breeding with slave women had become common but now the practice was openly encouraged. According to some estimates, in parts of the country, for every baby born in wedlock – for the slaves had also been encouraged to marry – there were over thirty illegitimate births. As the years went by, the slaves were worked harder and their retirement age was put back, so that it was not uncommon – but more so in the mining areas – for a man to be made to work until he literally dropped dead. The campaigners for total abolition worked hard but, again characteristically, one thing deterred them from pushing their efforts too far. That was the spectacle of the American civil war which was now raging. In 1865, with Brazil's declaration of war against Paraguay, the abolitionist campaign had to be halted for five years.

The war over, the campaign was resumed, and with even greater intensity, for now it was no longer the cause only of certain politicians and crusading abolitionists; it was becoming a popular crusade and it gradually inflamed the whole country. No issue had ever captured the imagination and the emotions of the ordinary Brazilian in quite the same way. This emotional approach to the problem achieved its object in the end; and yet, however inhumane it may sound to say this, it could be argued that, had the issue been less charged with emotion, certainly in its latter stages, the ultimate aim of the abolitionists, to put an end to the whole institution of slavery, might have been achieved differently and without the national disaster it caused.

Apart from the economic consequences to the country of the total and almost abrupt end of slavery, an entire class of Brazilians was condemned and alienated. The landowners, who were responsible for the basis of Brazil's economy, now found themselves pilloried as the personification of all evil. Was this justified? Many Brazilians today would have no hesitation in answering yes. But if one looks at this whole issue in the context of the times, the landowning class did not deserve perhaps quite so much condemnation. This vast country was virtually unpopulated; there was still no immigration, no alternative to slave labour. The landowners had inherited the institution of slavery from colonial days, and it was an institution which went back for over three centuries; and, again in the context of the times, they had treated their slave labour well. In some ways, these slaves fared better than the workers in the factories and in the mines in the advanced countries of Europe at that time. But the abolitionist campaign thundered on.

With the import of slaves now ended, the abolitionists turned their attention to stamping out the remaining source of slave labour: the children born of slave women. It was a measure which had been thought of by the Emperor himself, but it had been pigeon-holed on the outbreak of the Paraguayan war. It was left to Viscount Rio Branco to steer through parliament this even more controversial and explosive Bill, which was to achieve the freedom of all children born of slaves. It was a hard fight; in parliament the heated debate over this issue lasted for five tense months. The Emperor was absent in Europe and his daughter, Princess Isabel, was acting as Regent. On 28 September 1871 Rio Branco put before her an Act which became known as the Law of the Free Womb. It provided that all children born after the day on which it was signed would be free. Isabel, who was as devout an abolitionist as her father, was only too eager to sign it and parliament made it law. It is recorded that after she had signed the Act, she turned exultantly to one of her ministers, a member of the anti-abolitionist faction, and exclaimed: 'We have won!' The minister agreed, but added: 'You have won the game, but you have lost the Crown.'

The new law stipulated, however, that such children must serve the masters of their mothers for a period of twenty-one years. There was also a clause which provided that certain sums from national revenue should be set aside each year and allocated to the various provinces to enable them to assist slaves to buy their own freedom. The Emperor had already freed his slaves; so also had two Brazilian provinces, Amazonas and Ceará. After 1871 some landowners else, where did the same, but the abolitionists still faced tremendous opposition. The next step in their campaign, a law freeing all slaves over the age of sixty, was the undoing of successive cabinets; and it was only in 1885 that this law was finally passed. Meanwhile, a growing number of prominent Brazilians both in and out of parlia, ment were making the cause of abolition almost a religious crusade. Men like Rio Branco, Joaquim Nabuco, Rui Barbosa, Souza Dantas and a dozen others practically staked their political future on the issue. Castro Alves became regarded as the greatest Brazilian poet of his time, largely because of his abolitionist poems. In São Paulo, the campaign took an even more daring turn. Prominent figures in society formed underground movements not only to help runaway slaves but to organize mass escapes from the great estates. São Paulo was also the first province in the whole country to have the initiative and the foresight to encourage immigration from Europe before the abolition.

In the face of such a crusade and popular outcry, even some of the staunchest anti-abolitionists in parliament capitulated. The Act which finally abolished the entire institution of slavery in Brazil and which was passed by both Houses became known as the Golden Law. It had been signed on 13 May 1888, but not by the Emperor. Once again Princess Isabel was Regent. Her father, who was now sixty-three and had been ailing for some time, was undergoing treat, ment in Europe; and so it was Isabel who officially signed the Golden Law; and the death warrant of the Empire.

It would seem cruelly ironic that this essentially humane piece of legislation should have been so regarded. The Emperor enjoyed not only immense popularity among the mass of the people; almost every great statesman of his day had a deep respect for his personal qualities and they were qualities which have enshrined him in Brazil's history. The Church had come to resent him because of the challenge their authority had suffered over the affair of the bishops and free, masonry; and yet Pedro had not been wholly responsible for the way in which that issue had developed. He had certainly launched and had been the greatest inspirer of the abolitionist movement. But it was a movement which had captured the imagination and stirred the conscience of the great majority of Brazilians, including men who were to become prominent in the Republic; it could never have succeeded otherwise. The landowners turned against Pedro and openly switched their support to the republican cause in what seems to have been an act of pure reprisal. Yet their feelings are understand, able. Apart from the moral stigma they now bore, to them the economic consequences of abolition were disastrous. The Golden Law made absolutely no provision for any compensation for the labour they had suddenly lost. To them, this was the final stab in the back by the Crown. It could be argued that they had had plenty of time in which to do very much more to ensure the existence of alternative labour by encouraging immigration. The abolitionist campaign had lasted for almost fifty years, gathering momentum until it finally and inevitably triumphed. Yet it was only towards the end of the nineteenth century that immigration really began. In 1883 an attempt was made to bring in Chinese coolie labour, but it was dropped in the face of protests by the British government and public revolt at the idea in Brazil itself. Between 1884 and 1893 about 880,000 immigrants entered Brazil, but most of them arrived after the abolition and settled in São Paulo, Minas Gerais and in the far south, not in the plantation areas of the north where not so much new labour as a new spirit of enterprise was most needed, and one can see the consequences of this today.

One of the failings of so many Brazilians still seems to be a reluctance to face up to impending disaster until it practically smothers them. And yet, they have developed a remarkable resilience in crises; if one considers some of the calamities which have hit them, one can only come to the conclusion that in some way they have learnt almost to defy gravity. Such a calamity struck in 1888. When complete abolition seemed only a matter of time there were some attempts in parliament to avoid the whole burden of its cost falling

on the shoulders of the slave owners. But suggestions of compensation were drowned in the emotional outcry against them and parliament did not dare to defy it. In 1888 there were some 723,500 slaves
worth at that time, according to some estimates, the equivalent of
over £40,000,000. That was the immediate down payment of the
cost of abolition to the slave owners. But the entire economy of the
country was disrupted too. Even though abolition did not mean that
slaves everywhere simply got up and walked away, a large proportion
of the great estates, the sugar plantations and cattle ranches, were
abandoned.

The reaction of the slaves and the immediate consequences to them
of emancipation were just as predictable. For some time the prospect
of freedom had no longer been just a bewildering dream. They knew
that abolition was on the way; but when it came, many of them
were not able to cope with it either. The older slaves seem to have
been almost phlegmatic about it all, but for the younger ones it was
a confusing, exhilarating moment. And yet, one fact perhaps sums
up their reaction to freedom not very long afterwards, the reaction to
the disillusionment and the hardships which they were now experiencing as free men. Many of them returned to the plantations and
the sugar mills, even to the mines which they had abandoned. The
process of adaptation to the new relationship between master and
man began, and, like so many of Brazil's revolutionary processes, it
was not so very long before everyone settled down in the new pattern.
Slavery had been abolished; but in many ways only in name.

Admittedly, the new status of Brazilian labour had been founded
at almost the lowest possible level. But it was a status which was to
persist for decades. Employers now tended to show less consideration
for their paid workers than they had for their slaves. In fact, it was
only in the 1930s – almost fifty years after the abolition – that
Brazilian labour was given such elementary legal protection as some
limitation of working hours, or any sort of provision for sickness or
old age. By paying often a barely subsistence wage, many an
employer divested himself of all responsibility for the welfare of his
workers. After the abolition of slavery a new kind of poverty and
defencelessness was born; and even today one can see more than just

a remnant of this indifference, not only in those dispirited, forgotten communities of the interior but in the slums and shanty towns of Brazil's great cities.

Pedro II returned to Brazil five months after the signing of the Golden Law to find a country in turmoil. Although his personal popularity among the mass of the people was perhaps even greater, in other quarters he was surrounded by the heavy air of hostility. The Emperor was a sick man and it was obvious from his behaviour during that last year of his reign that he realized the Empire could not survive. He seems to have been far more sure of this than many of the monarchists who were still loyal to him, for some of them sincerely believed that, for the sake of the country, the Empire must continue, at least for a time. These men did realize that feelings were against the Crown, not only due to the resentment which it had aroused but because, to many Brazilians, the régime now stood in archaic isolation in an entirely republican continent; but they still wanted to postpone the transition. The Emperor, however, did nothing to forestall or even delay the end. The remaining pillar of the régime, the army, had not yet collapsed but it was crumbling fast, much faster than many monarchists realized at the time.

There was another factor, although a minor contributory one, against the continuation of the Empire. Pedro II had married an Italian of royal blood, Dona Cristina, and there were four children of this match. But Pedro's two sons had died and he would have been succeeded by his eldest daughter, Isabel. Apart from her role in the process of abolition, Brazilians had acquired a deep dislike for her husband, the Compte d'Eu, 'that arrogant and insolent Frenchman', as Brazilians called him. Nevertheless, the monarchists had hoped that the Empire would survive at least until the Emperor's death.

But the alliance between the army and the republican forces had been growing closer even before the ultimate explosion of anti-monarchist feeling in 1888. To this alliance was added the less overt, but emotion and conscience stirring support of the Church. The manner in which the army took over the role of executioner of the régime, the role of supreme arbitrator in crises between governments and opposition, set a pattern which was to be followed time and again in the future. On the night of 15 November 1889 the republican plot, carefully conceived and quietly executed, ended the Empire. The Republic was proclaimed and Dom Pedro II and his entire family were exiled two days later. The reaction of the ordinary Brazilian was one of shock. Even some members of the government were stunned by the suddenness of events. But there was no other reaction, no attempt to put up even a symbolic resistance to the revolution as a testimonial to a man and a régime which had done so much for the country. Not even his own chaplain, the Bishop of Rio, had a word of sympathy for Pedro or his family at the moment of their banishment into exile. And yet this was not just the end of a régime and the, surely undeserved, ignominious exile of its head almost on the eve of his Golden Jubilee. It was the death of an era, perhaps one of the most significant in Brazil's history, in men and ideals, and it died without a whimper.

Subsequent accounts of those last days anxiously stress that the Emperor and his family were allowed to leave the country in perfect safety; that, although his property in Brazil had been seized, the new government, appreciating that Pedro had almost no means of support, voted him a pension of approximately £500 a year, which he refused. Two years later he died in a second-rate hotel in Paris. But the Brazilians' sense of guilt had been growing deeper and in 1922, to mark the celebrations of the first centenary of independence, the Imperial family were allowed to return to Brazil and much of their property was restored to them. The body of Dom Pedro II was brought home too, to be buried in the Cathedral at Petrópolis in the mountains near Rio where the descendants of the Imperial family still live.

7   Republican Brazil

THE TRANSITION FROM MONARCHY to Republic was inevitable. Quite apart from the personal resentments which had been aroused during the Second Empire, a republican form of government was far more compatible with the mood of the times. And yet, might it not have been better for Brazil if the transition had not been quite so sudden? Pedro himself might have been only too willing to have presided as a stabilizing influence over a period of preparation for the Republic. But one section of Brazilians were impatient for the change and their motives were not entirely altruistic. This was the army.

It is true that the advent of the Republic marked a decisive step forward in the emancipation of Brazil as a nation. But it can also be argued that what the first Republic did was very largely to carry on a process which had already begun during the Second Empire. It did not initiate it. Furthermore, before Brazil took those giant strides forward, as the new republican architects liked to claim she did only after the fall of the Empire, the country slipped back into another period of political pandemonium and economic crisis; and the cause of the latter was not only the consequences of the abolition of slavery. It was due to extravagance, mismanagement and the resurgence of corruption during the military governments which succeeded the old régime. It was only after 1930, but even more so after the Second World War, that Brazil really took those giant strides.

In the latter years of the Republic, Brazil's somewhat confused political party system was also born. Previously there had been factions, loose groupings of men with broadly the same ideas. The politicians were divided, again rather loosely, between conservatives and liberals, the latter with rather less clearly defined aims. Although both these factions regarded the army as the common opponent, the conservatives in particular were not loath to turn to the military for support on occasions. What has injected an element of even greater confusion in the party system is that, as the electorate grew from a few thousand in the very early days of the Republic to almost 19 million in 1964, ordinary Brazilians at election times have tended to be more attracted by personalities than by parties. Although there are large and organized parties, their policies are not always very positively defined. Well aware of the Brazilian cult of personalities in politics, they will sometimes split up into a bewildering set of factions in support of likely candidates, even though they may belong to other parties. The one truly disciplined political body in the country, although it is outlawed, is the Communist Party, and its support is often courted by conservative candidates too. Even Brazilian commentators can get lost in the maze of shifting political loyalties at election times.

But the Republic also witnessed the emergence of a factor which was to play an important role in Brazilian affairs ever after. It was the consolidation of a new *élite*, the military *élite*. In latter years the Brazilian armed forces were to play a highly responsible and stabiliz-ing role in the periodic conflicts between civilian political factions. In fact, it has been thanks to the influence of a level-headed majority of military leaders that Brazil has been snatched from civil war on more than one occasion. But in the last years of the Empire and during the early part of the Republic the army saw itself as the logical inheritor, if not of absolute power, at least of a right to play a far greater role in political affairs. Much of this confidence and the feeling that it had earned this right of direction was due to the Paraguayan war, when the army had certainly distinguished itself. During those five years the armed forces suffered over 30,000 casual-ties. But men like Caxias and Deodoro da Fonseca, who led the revolt against the Emperor, had also given the army a new spirit and a new pride. The influx of recruits during the war had also broken down the barriers which had existed between the youth of the country and the traditional officer class and both found that they had much in common. Although the leaders of the military conspiracy which established the Republic were older men, the spirit of revolt in the army, the desire for change, was essentially a youthful spirit.

But the armed forces also had a feeling of personal resentment against the Emperor which sprang from almost the same root as the antagonism of the Church. Pedro had no great respect for the military mentality. Perhaps because of his essentially civilian education, but even more so because he was fundamentally a pacifist, he could not understand the military mind. To him, the army as an institution was a necessary evil, but not one to be pandered to, certainly in peace-time. Soldiers, he felt, should keep to their barracks and he was frequently at loggerheads with his military commanders or would-be military advisers whenever they seemed to show signs of wanting to intrude in the affairs of government. To the soldiers, this sort of attitude was, in its simplest interpretation, rank ingratitude. Not only had they quelled the revolts in the provinces against the Emperor and the Central government, they had just defended the nation itself in a long and bloody war, to say nothing of the campaign against Argentina. Now the Emperor was denying them their rightful place among his counsellors. The alliance between the military and the civilian republican forces and other disaffected elements in the country was a natural development. But once the Republic was installed, the military leaders were quick to remind their civilian co-plotters who it was that had actually made it possible. The seeds of discord and often open conflict between the military and the civilian powers had been planted and it was a long time before these two factions were able to agree on some form of coexistence; but a certain tension still exists between the two.

In most Latin American countries the army is usually far more united than any political party or faction. Often it is the only disciplined organization, quite apart from the fact that it has the means to implant its ideas. The army is also the senior service, and it feels that by tradition it should be the leader of the armed forces as a whole. There are inter-service rivalries, of course, and one of the greatest challengers of the army's leadership has become the air force. By virtue of the superior education, training and social background

Political map of Brazil

of its members, this relatively new branch of the services has come to regard itself as a new military *élite* with ideals and ambitions of its own. Most South American navies, on the other hand, were formed and trained by the British and they still retain something of British traditions. They consider themselves to be more select than the army and less brash than the air force.

All this applies in Brazil too, yet the Brazilian armed forces have been able to develop and maintain a remarkably united front in times of crisis. In any political conflict all factions turn to the armed forces in the same way as warring nations conscript the Almighty. What makes the army still fume is that the politicians are quick to invoke their help in these crises and then, when the trouble is over, expect the soldiers to return meekly to their barracks. While almost all Brazilians deplore the army's role of police dog they have come to realize, reluctantly, that it is necessary; and this role has become all the more important since Brazilian politics entered a new and convulsive phase of experiment and adaptation following the Vargas social revolution of 1930, and again with the advent of the Cuban revolution in 1959. Today, the Brazilian armed forces, providing they remain united, are perhaps the greatest defence a great many Brazilians have against their own impulsiveness and political immaturity and against the excesses and demagogy of so many of Brazil's new politicians. When one looks back to the army's behaviour during the first years of the Republic, and even later, in the days of the Vargas dictatorship, for example, it is remarkable that the military should have evolved and matured so quickly into the stabilizing force, the 'class apart', which it is today.

The first Republican government was to be a provisional military one. At least, that is what the civilian architects of the new régime had intended it to be. It had been planned, as so many other Brazilian revolts have been since, during long discussions between the civilian and military factions of the republican conspiracy. The details were finally agreed at a secret gathering in the house of Marshal Manuel Deodoro da Fonseca, the head of the armed forces, four days before the ultimatum demanding the Emperor's abdication was delivered to him on the night of 15 November. Pedro was presiding over a meeting of the Cabinet which at the time was seeking ways to lessen the dissatisfaction in the army. Their proposals were to have been put before parliament which was due to assemble on 20 November. But even as they discussed these grievances, troops were surrounding the palace. On that night, Deodoro da Fonseca became head of the provisional government. The army was to retain control of the government until 1894; and it regained control, in somewhat dubious circumstances, for another and disastrous period of four years, in 1910.

Deodoro da Fonseca remained provisional head until 1891 when he became Brazil's first president. In February of that year the constituent assembly which he had summoned introduced Brazil's new constitution. There had been a movement to fashion this on British lines, but in the end, to emphasize the republican spirit in the country, it was modelled closely on the constitution of the United States of America. It provided for an elected Senate and a Chamber of Deputies and gave wide executive powers to the president. It was a federal constitution, and although the states retained many of their administrative rights, the Federal government was empowered to intervene in a number of circumstances. This constitution, which provided for freedom of speech and of the press, the separation of Church and State, freedom of worship, the institution of civil marriage, trial by jury and the abolition of the death penalty, remained in force until the advent of the Vargas dictatorship in the 1930s.

But Deodoro da Fonseca had as much understanding of constitutional government as Pedro II had of the military mind. He was constantly in conflict with his civilian advisers and later with Congress. He insisted on keeping intact a ministry which had become increasingly unpopular. On 3 November, just nine months after his solemn acceptance of the new constitution, impatient with Congress and backed by the army, he dissolved it and proclaimed himself dictator. But already there was a spark of a feeling of responsibility and propriety in the army, and opposition to this act of contempt for the constitution was such that less than three weeks later he resigned in favour of the vice-president, Marshal Floriano

Peixoto. Floriano had been another of the military leaders of the conspiracy against the Emperor and his respect for constitutional procedure was just as scanty. Admittedly, to the military mind the wrangling of the politicians and their apparent lack of respect for a uniform must have been exasperating, but Floriano also went too far in asserting his authority. In 1893 a naval revolt which was joined by army units broke out and it took a year before it was put down.

In 1894 the first civilian was elected president. He was Prudente José de Moraes Barros, a lawyer, and he was from São Paulo. He was the first of a succession of Paulistas to govern the country, for already, thanks to its economic progress, São Paulo was becoming a new political influence. For a time, it seemed as if Floriano had no intention of relinquishing power to 'this civilian lawyer', but he did not have the support he had obviously expected from his colleagues; and so, on 15 November 1894, Prudente de Moraes took office. A great many Brazilians heaved a sigh of relief. But it was not the end of the army's determination to call the political tune.

Prudente de Moraes was a republican of long standing and he had had a distinguished career in São Paulo. There was no doubting his good intentions or his ability. He was also determined to curtail the military influence in the government. He dismissed a number of officers who had been appointed to civilian posts and very soon he found himself at war with the army. The military systematically harassed his government and during his four-year term of office he was faced with a succession of distracting military or military-inspired risings in different parts of the country. At the end of his government, Brazil's finances, too, were almost on the point of collapse. In 1898 Prudente de Moraes was succeeded by another Paulista, Manoel Ferraz de Campos Salles, who had been president of the state of São Paulo. Campos Salles distinguished himself as the man who saved Brazil from bankruptcy. The country was facing its first real financial crisis, thanks to the extravagant spending, the speculation and an inflated currency which had followed the over-throw of the Empire; and the situation had been aggravated by the almost constant political turmoil. Even before he took office, Campos Salles negotiated a funding loan with the Rothschilds of £10,000,000.

The new president was an able administrator, and even though he had stood in opposition to a military candidate, he was more fortu-nate, and more adroit, than Prudente de Moraes had been in his relationship with the army. His election was also significant, as it showed not only a greater strength of the civilian political machine but the growing resentment to soldiers in politics. During his govern-ment, Brazil also demonstrated her remarkable recuperative powers, that resilience in crisis which has been a feature of her economy and her politics ever since.

Brazil's third civilian president, Francisco de Paula Rodrigues Alves, was also a Paulista, and one of the most able presidents Brazil has ever had. He took office in 1902 and the success of his govern-ment in foreign affairs, particularly in achieving a final solution of some long-standing boundary disputes, was largely due to the diplo-macy of the Foreign Minister, Baron Rio Branco, the son of Viscount Rio Branco of the days of the Second Empire. He and his father laid the foundations of Brazil's foreign policy, including that 'sacred principle' of non-interference in the affairs of others which has been the golden rule of Brazil's foreign relations since 1870. Rodrigues Alves's government was also responsible for one of the most remark-able campaigns against disease to be carried out anywhere in the world. This began with the work of a young Brazilian doctor, Oswaldo Cruz, a former student of Pasteur, to rid Rio de Janeiro of yellow fever. It was the periodic scourge not only of the capital but of other Brazilian towns. This campaign revealed a quality of tenacity and a genius for improvisation in certain Brazilians and they are qualities which they show to a remarkable degree when they are engaged on something which has really captured their imagina-tion. The yellow fever campaign lasted for over forty years. It often lacked funds and the teams of 'mosquito hunters', as they were derisively called, usually had to work with primitive and makeshift equipment and in the teeth of the ignorance and the often violent obstruction from the people even in the towns. But they succeeded in stamping out the fever, first in Rio and later in other centres, and even in the more remote settlements of the interior. It was during Rodrigues Alves's government that Rio, now free of fever, began to be transformed into what Brazilians still call the 'Enchanted City'.

As the next presidential campaign drew near, political factions in a number of Brazilian states joined forces to break the monopoly of the presidency which São Paulo now seemed to have acquired. After long discussions, a compromise candidate from Minas Gerais was chosen. He was Afonso Augusto Moreira Pena and in 1906 he was duly elected president. Brazilian elections were not exactly a mockery, but by no stretch of the imagination could they be said to reflect the will of the people. The electorate represented a very small element of the population and in a variety of ways voting could be, and was, controlled. It had become the rule that a candidate supported by the outgoing government was automatically assured of victory. In fact, it was the rule for years to come, so much so that candidates hardly bothered to campaign outside political circles. The election of Afonso Pena might seem to have been a break in this rule, but in actual fact the government election machine was only to suffer its first defeat fifty-five years later, in 1961, with the election of Janio Quadros, an independent, although in 1930 Vargas seized, rather than won power. Afonso Pena's government was by no means undistinguished. He, too, concentrated his efforts on financial matters, for it was a subject with which Brazilians were becoming increasingly concerned as their economy, now very largely based on São Paulo's coffee, steadily expanded. Afonso Pena not only overhauled the national economy, he took the first important step towards stabilization of exchange by creating a Conversion Bank. The outbreak of the First World War, however, and a further period of mismanagement and extravagance, although this time it was a civilian and not a military government which was responsible, were to bring the country's economy to its knees again. But long before this, in 1909, Afonso Pena died and he was succeeded for the remaining year of what should have been his term by the vice-president, Nilo Peçanha.

In 1910 military government returned to Brazil, and it was thanks to civilian politicians that it did so. The popular candidate at that time was Rui Barbosa, a northerner and another of the old republican school who, even in the days of the Second Empire, had enjoyed tremendous prestige as a writer and a brilliant lawyer. He was now acknowledged as one of the wise men of his time with an international outlook and an enlightened, liberal approach to his country's problems. Confronted with such a formidable opponent, conservative political leaders turned to the one faction they were sure could save them: the army. They chose as their candidate Marshal Hermes da Fonseca, the nephew of Deodoro, who had been Brazil's first president in the stormy, early days of the Republic. Even those elements in the army who were becoming sensitive to such public opinion as there was could hardly withhold their support of such a candidate; it was not just a matter of loyalty, military honour was at stake. Hermes da Fonseca was also officially endorsed by the outgoing government and in these circumstances his election was a foregone conclusion. He took office in a cloud of bitterness and amid a clamour of cries of fraud. Soon afterwards, the navy revolted, and it all set the tone of events during the next four years. Much of the work, but particularly the new standards which the three civilian governments had achieved in twelve years were very largely destroyed in less than four.

The clouds of the First World War were still gathering blackly over Europe when Brazil began to prepare for the next election in 1914. This time the liberals and the anti-militarists were determined not to be 'cheated'. Their candidate was again Rui Barbosa. It was almost generally accepted that in the 1910 election he had received a majority and that Hermes da Fonseca had not been elected but appointed by the government machine. The liberals were certain that this time Barbosa would get a majority which would be hard to defy. But Barbosa knew that the campaign would be a bitter and dangerous one. Brazil was again in economic trouble, the price of coffee had dropped heavily and by this time Brazil was supplying about 70 per cent of the world's coffee. The rubber trade was also suffering the effects of the competition of Asiatic production and Barbosa realized that the country could not stand a political crisis as well, and so he withdrew. A compromise candidate was found in Wenceslao Braz Pereira Gomes, a former president of Minas Gerais; and with Barbosa's blessing, and almost everyone else's approval, he was elected and took office three months after the outbreak of the First World War.

Ever since the early days of the Empire, Brazilians had shown a deep interest in the outside world, but it was during Wenceslao Braz's government that she made her first entry into international affairs. From the very first, Brazilian sympathies were with Britain and her Allies. The remarkable thing was that even the growing German community in the south felt the same. The Minister of Foreign Affairs, Lauro Müller, who was of pure German descent, openly sided with Britain even though Brazil, following the policy laid down by the United States for the whole continent, was officially neutral. Within a month of the outbreak of war the Chamber of Deputies was condemning Germany and in 1915 Rui Barbosa founded the Brazilian League for aiding the Allies and was rebuking the United States for not having rallied the Americas against Germany because of her invasion of Belgium. Brazil declared war on Germany on 26 October 1917, six months after the United States had officially entered the war, but her neutrality had been broken long before. Her contribution to the Allied cause was understandably small. She sent part of her fleet – a Brazilian warship helped to patrol the west coast of Africa – and she also dispatched a medical mission to the Western Front. Her main contribution was the supply of food and raw materials. But the war, and Brazil's modest but whole-hearted contribution to its outcome, had a psychological effect on the Brazilians. Brazil participated in the peace conference and was given a seat on the Council of the League of Nations, and Brazilians felt a glow of pride to think that now they had the right to sit at the top table of nations.

In the election of 1918 Rodrigues Alves, whose government had been such a success, was elected again. But he was a sick man and died before his inauguration. The presidency therefore passed to Delfim Moreira da Costa Ribeiro, the vice-president. A new election was held less than a year later and in June 1919 Epitacio da Silva Pessôa took office. He, too, was a distinguished lawyer and had led the Brazilian delegation at Versailles. He was also the first and only northerner ever to be elected president.

Brazil in those post-war years was in a jubilant mood of expansion. The economy was experiencing a boom, industrialization was thriving, and the Brazilians were also preparing to celebrate the first centenary of their independence. The lavishness and the cost of the great Brazilian Centenary Exhibition of 1922 epitomized the extra-vagant mood of those years and Brazil's internal and foreign debts rose accordingly. It was the same sort of mood which President Kubitscheck was to inspire almost forty years later, in 1956, and with much the same consequences. Brazilians then were being dazzled by the galloping pace of their industrialization and the spectacle of the building of Brasilia. Again they felt a sense of elation that their country was acquiring a new stature in the world.

Nevertheless, during Epitacio Pessôa's government, some important public works were begun. In the drought region of the northeast an irrigation and water conservation scheme was started but the slump which was soon to come caught up with them all. Under the constitution, Epitacio Pessôa could only govern for three years to complete the 1918–22 term of office which should have been served by Rodrigues Alves. When the time for a new election came round, Brazil was not only in deep financial trouble, the rumbles of one of the longest political storms the country had ever known could be clearly heard. It was a crisis which was to reach its climax eight years later with the advent of the Vargas régime and that was an upheaval in some ways greater, and which certainly had more far-reaching effects than the fall of the Empire.

By now, the choice of presidents had begun to follow a pattern; São Paulo and Minas Gerais took it in turn to put up successive candidates. It was a compromise between what had become the two principal political forces in the country and both represented the great landed interests. Epitacio Pessôa, from Paraiba, had been an exception which the king-makers had accepted. Rui Barbosa, the 'defeated' candidate in the election of 1910, was from Bahia in the north. Of the fourteen *elected* civilian presidents, eleven were either from Minas or São Paulo. It was no surprise, therefore, to the hitherto docile electorate when the official candidate in the 1922 election was announced. He was Arthur da Silva Bernardes from

Minas Gerais. He was elected and took office to an even louder chorus of protest than had greeted Hermes da Fonseca's victory over Rui Barbosa. Military and civilian supporters of the opposition candidate, Nilo Peçanha, the former interim president after the death of Afonso Pena and who, incidentally, was from Rio de Janeiro, openly charged the government with fraud. There was an armed attempt to prevent Bernardes from taking office; and, later, the revolts and political tension were such that he declared a state of emergency which he had to maintain throughout most of his term of office. Many of his opponents undoubtedly had an axe to grind, but many also attacked him in a sincere attempt to destroy what they felt to be a new and dangerously unconstitutional oligarchy. The mass of Brazilians were also in a state of revolt. What they could see was a succession of governments which had come to power thanks to the efforts of purely political and economic interests that seemed to take little interest in the plight of ordinary people; and these people were undoubtedly undergoing a great deal of hardship now.

Some of the economy measures which the Bernardes government was taking to fight the financial crisis, the suspension of public works and the effects on prices of new taxation, were obviously necessary but they did not add to its popularity. The irrigation schemes in the northeast, for example, which had been started by Epitacio Pessôa, were abandoned and ordinary Brazilians felt that too much of the burden of these remedies was being put on the shoulders of people whose resources were already strained to the limit. What they asked themselves was, whether everyone was having to make sacrifices too. Brazilians were in a confused and ugly mood and the resentment against the politicians and the vested interests who, they felt, had manipulated them like puppets for so long, grew and to some degree it still persists today. In the election of 1926 Bernardes was succeeded by Washington Luiz Pereira de Souza, and in conformity with the pattern he was from São Paulo. Washington Luiz was an able administrator and he did a great deal to pacify the country; so much so, that within a year of taking office he was able to lift the state of emergency. But he could not avert the great depression of the late twenties. Now the world price not just of coffee but of every Brazilian exportable commodity slumped. The new industries were hit too, and 1929 witnessed the demoralizing spectacle of bankruptcies, a ruined agriculture and mounting un/ employment. The scene was set for what was to be the finale of the first Republic and all that it stood for. Ironically, it was the conserva/ tive politicians who jerked the curtain up and so precipitated the last act.

According to the rules, in the election of 1930 the government should have put up a candidate from Minas Gerais. Instead, Washington Luiz insisted on supporting another Paulista, Julio Prestes, a conservative who had been president of the state of São Paulo and a man of proven administrative ability. At a time when Brazil was undergoing serious economic difficulties, Washington Luiz argued that this ability was a far more important qualification than political credentials. It is true that Washington Luiz was also influenced by personal feelings and by Paulista economic interests. But São Paulo, with its coffee, was the pillar of the country's economy and the Paulistas felt, as the army had done forty years before, that they had the right to a say in the country's affairs, parti/ cularly at such a time. And it is possible that Prestes, backed by the influence and the economic resources of São Paulo, might have had a fair chance of steering Brazil through the crisis. But the govern/ ment's political support was split wide open over this breach of convention. The *Mineiros* in particular were outraged and it all demonstrated just how torn Brazilians were, and to some extent they still are, between national and regional loyalties. But there was also a resurgence of liberal feelings and of protest against the government's role of king/maker which resulted in a somewhat confused alliance of ideals and interests.

The opposition group in the government circle joined the Mineiros and liberal factions in the search for a likely candidate, and they almost split again over the choice between two men: João Pessôa, a northerner, and Getulio Vargas from Rio Grande in the south. In the end, Vargas stood as the candidate of the new alliance, the *Aliança Liberal*. Nevertheless Julio Pestes, the government candi/ date, was elected, and again to the now familiar chant of protest. But this time, Brazilians were not so philosophical in defeat. Vargas, supported by the army, led a revolution which met with little opposition except from the Paulistas, and Washington Luiz was overthrown before he could hand over to Julio Prestes. Vargas ruled Brazil for fifteen years, most of the time as dictator, and he was to return, this time as an elected president, in 1951.

Vargas was not exactly a political independent but a great many Brazilians regarded him as such simply because they felt that he was not committed to the traditional political and economic clique. To some extent this was true, although very soon he was to create his own clique which was to become just as dominating. It was this belief in his independence and the faith they still had in him as the champion of the under-privileged which prompted so many of them to vote for him in 1951. On the day he took office people knelt in the streets as his car went by as if they were watching a religious procession. The Vargas era not only changed the political system of a country, it transformed the mentality of almost an entire people. Vargas was certainly a new and brutal architect and he began by destroying much of that philosophical apathy with which so many Brazilians had accepted the disparity of lots. Yet, characteristically, they never exploded into the violence and the excesses of class hatred as the Argentine masses did when Juan Perón inspired much the same sort of revolt in Argentina.

Like many other Latin American dictators in recent times, from Juan Perón to Fidel Castro in Cuba, Vargas owed his success not to any specially great talents or great policies but to the lack of imagination and the greediness of minorities. But they all collapsed because these men, pushed into leadership by force of circumstances, were not big enough to fill their roles. Yet the under-privileged Brazilians still see in Vargas something which they had never seen in any of their previous leaders; a man who had pledged himself to be the champion of the underdog. Their great expectations were not all fulfilled, by any means, but so little had been done for them in the past that although what Vargas gave them in the way of social security, for example, might seem elementary, it was nevertheless revolutionary. He was the first man really to stir the hearts of that great majority of Brazilians whose plight the ruling minority seemed to have forgotten all about. And the Vargas legend lives on: Vargas, the Father of the Poor, the Champion of the Little Man. Few men have earned such accolades so easily and even when he failed to fulfil promises, even when he committed suicide in the cloud of unsavoury dust in which his last government crashed in 1954, many Brazilians could not find it in their hearts to blame him. Instead, they blamed the men around him; the traditional ruling classes. They even blamed 'scheming foreign interests', but never 'our Getulio', as he is still affectionately remembered. But even Vargas had not been able to eradicate the virus of poverty in the country. In the northeast and in the interior a handful of landlords still controlled the destiny of millions of landless peasants and they still do.

Could another man like him, or even a Fidel Castro, succeed in the same emotional way in Brazil today? Perhaps he could, and for much the same reasons which opened the way for Vargas, although obviously it would not be so easy. In the decades since independence, Brazil has evolved, somewhat jerkily, both economically and politi/ cally into one of the most advanced countries of Latin America, and her prospects in a changing world seem as infinite and as rich as her vast empty interior. But in some ways the evolution of the Brazilians, although it has been remarkable, has not progressed in the same way. One still tends to think of them as a young people, although Brazil has existed as a sovereign nation for almost 150 years – only fifty/six years less than the United States. Yet a very great many Brazilians still live in conditions which belong to the nineteenth century. In 1930, on the eve of the Vargas era, a new Brazilian had already emerged, the result of a new blending not of races but of national/ ities which had come in on the tide of immigration which began after the fall of the Empire forty/one years earlier. In the first year of the Republic, Brazil had a population of 14 million; now it was almost 34 million, and 1930 is a good starting/point at which to begin a study of how the Brazilian had evolved up to then and how he has evolved ever since.

30 Panning for gold. Gold was first discovered in Minas Gerais by the *Bandeirantes* in 1693.

31 Diamonds were discovered in 1727. A group of diamond miners in the eighteenth century. Both engravings of the nineteenth century by J. M. Rugendas.

32 Brazil's economy depended heavily on slave labour. A nineteenth-century print of a slave market in Rio de Janeiro.

33 Over a million slaves were imported from Africa. A nineteenth-century print of a slave ship.

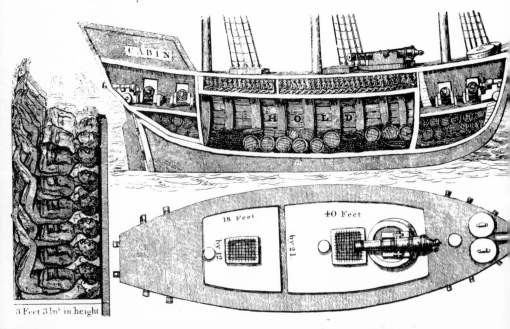

3 Feet 3 In³ in height

18 Feet

40 Feet

34 By the nineteenth century, when Rugendas made these two engravings, the Catholic faith had taken its own form among the Negroes.

35 A plantation family of the period. Landowners were, and still are, the pillars of Brazil's economy.

36 In the days of the Empire, the Constitution provided for a Chamber of Deputies which already aimed at a form of democratic government. A nineteenth-century print.

37 But real power was in the hands of the Senate which could dissolve the Chamber of Deputies and suspend legislation. A nineteenth-century print of the Senate House.

38 Brazil's rubber trade boomed during the nineteenth century. Primitive manu,
facture of rubber shoes, from a contemporary print.

39 Chinese, and later Japanese, started the first tea plantations such as this one.
From an engraving by Rugendas.

40 After Brazil became a republic in 1889, considerable progress was made in science and
medicine. Oswaldo Cruz (1872–
1917) was responsible for the
successful campaign to rid Rio de
Janeiro of yellow fever.

41 General Cândido Rondon
(1865–1958), famous for his work
among the Indians, seen here with
members of the primitive Nhambi-
quiara tribe.

42, 43 Coffee and sugar are Brazil's most important crops. *Right*, a first stage in cleaning coffee beans before washing and drying. *Left*, cutting sugar cane in Pernambuco.

44 Coffee beans are laid out on great cemented drying beds such as at this São Paulo coffee farm.

45 Pôrto Alégre, capital of the state of Rio Grande and the industrial centre of the far south.

8 The Brazilian

FROM THE TIME the Brazilians began to be distinguishable as a people, they could be divided into two broad groups: the white and the coloured. Although this is still the main division, since the beginning of the twentieth century Brazilians can also in another sense be divided, again very broadly, into two: those whose ancestry is Portuguese and those who are descended from the non-Portuguese immigrant. The rich minority of the Portuguese-descended Brazilians carry on the traditions of the old aristocracy and although some of these old families have also gone into industry, which has created another economic *élite*, their fortunes and mentality are still largely based on the land. The traditional diplomatic, political and military hierarchies also have their roots in this strata.

The new non-Portuguese Brazilians have obviously no such traditions, and on the whole they are more progressive in their outlook and rather less extravagantly nationalistic. Their fathers or grandfathers came to Brazil in the nineteenth and twentieth centuries often as poor as the Portuguese immigrants who arrived with them, yet they have already built some of the largest industrial and commercial undertakings in the country. This type of Brazilian has also contributed far less to that vast layer at the foot of the social and economic ladder.

A further division of Brazilians could be made today into the two categories of builders and spectators, and thinking Brazilians agree that the former need reinforcements badly. When one considers the roots of the poverty and the reasons for the inertia of those growing millions who live on the fringe of the building site, it is only too easy to appreciate just how desperate the need is to raise the standards of

living of this other Brazil. But meanwhile, one solution to the problem of development of the country as a whole would seem to be
more immigration, not only directed to areas where it is most needed
but actively encouraged when it gets there.

Although Brazil is now among the ten most populated countries
in the world, the lack of the right people has been one of the features
of this subcontinent of a country ever since the early days of colonization more than four centuries ago. The first Portuguese settlers found
a vast land – and it took them over a hundred years to appreciate just
how vast it was – thinly populated by primitive Indians. In the
sixteenth century Portugal herself had a very small population,
which would seem out of all proportion to the extent of her overseas
ventures, and the Portuguese who chose to go out into the world to
seek their fortunes were not attracted by the unknown and apparently
worthless, empty land of Brazil. Those who did come, certainly in
the first decades after her discovery, were not the best that Portugal
could export.

For over three hundred years Brazil as a Portuguese colony was
isolated from the rest of the world as far as immigration was concerned. Her aboriginal population was made up of scattered Indian
communities all branching from four or five main tribes and they
were mostly a nomadic people who had not achieved anything like
the degree of culture of the Indian of the westerly part of Spanish
America. Although some tribes wove and produced rough earthen-
ware and cultivated crops, others had not reached the stage of using
implements. Few of them, in fact, had advanced very far beyond the
basic struggle to find food each day. The Indian population at the
time of the discovery has been estimated as about eight hundred
thousand. It is a figure usually quoted in official Brazilian reference
books, although it must be a very rough estimate indeed, for even
today it is not known precisely how many of these aboriginals still
exist in the remote wilds of Amazonia and Mato Grosso. The
official estimate of the pure Indian population today is 150,000. In
the sixteenth century the Indians who survived slaughter and the
white man's diseases were enslaved. In parts of Brazil, however,
particularly in the north and in the south in what is today the state

of São Paulo, the early settlers intermarried freely with the Indian, producing a distinctive type, the *Mamelucos*, which is still clearly discernible in many old Paulista families, the descendants of those early Brazilian explorers the *Bandeirantes*. In the north, the mameluco strain has survived in the tenacious people of the parched lands of the Sertões, in the interior of Brazil's northeast. The Indians also intermarried with the Negroes to produce another distinctive, although not so numerous type, the *Cafuso*. But the Indians were no solution to the labour problem of the early settlers.

As the colony slowly progressed, but even more so after the discovery of gold in 1693, this problem became increasingly acute and the Portuguese solution was the inevitable one of the times: to bring in slaves from Africa. They came from the Sudan, the Congo and from the Portuguese colonies, but just how many is not really known. It is fairly reliably estimated, however, that in the thirty years up to 1855, when Brazil, already independent for thirty-three years, abolished the slave trade, over 1,500,000 slaves were brought in. But long before this, owing to the lack of immigration and the relatively small number of Portuguese settlers, Brazil was a predominantly negroid country. Even in 1818, four years before independence, it was estimated by Humboldt, after his travels around South America, that of Brazil's population of 3,600,000, almost 2,500,000 were either pure Negroes or of mixed descent. According to this same estimate, which Brazilian authorities accept as a fairly accurate indication of the racial composition at the time, the Indian population was about 260,000. White accounted for just over 840,000.

This mixture was to be the ethnological basis of the Brazilians as people for almost four hundred years after her discovery, for it was only in 1890 that the stream of European immigration really began. But even this was a trickle compared to the swollen river of new blood which poured into the United States, for example. In the century after her independence in 1822, fewer than 4 million Europeans came to Brazil; in those same hundred years over 33 million settled in the United States. In fact, in three years, between 1905 and 1908, the United States received almost as many immigrants as Brazil did in a whole century.

Brazil, although increasingly conscious of her great empty spaces, has never really encouraged immigrants in the same way as other countries with the same problem have done, and are still doing. Although she is experiencing a population explosion the great con/centration of her people is to be found in a relatively small area of the country, but even that area is vast enough to support a great many more. And there are other areas, not inhospitable or even very remote which only await people and enterprise to bring them to life. Some Brazilian and foreign authorities maintain that even without calling upon the land and the unknown resources of the deep interior, Brazil today might have had a population of three hundred million. Others claim that Brazil could support a population of seven hundred million, if only development and colonization could be more co/ordinated and far/sighted.

Yet even today, the foreigner is not welcomed with any enthu/siasm, particularly by the Brazilian of Portuguese descent. Brazilian suspicions of foreigners are reflected in their attitude to the immigrant to such an extent, for example, that although the country is desper/ately short of doctors in rural areas, a foreign doctor may not practise in Brazil. Even foreign technicians, which she also needs so badly can experience endless difficulties and irritations. All the liberal professions are closed to foreigners, almost as if the Brazilians, in a display of that peculiar inferiority complex, are afraid that they will somehow outsmart the local talent. The sort of immigrant the Brazilian wants is the man who is prepared to go into the interior and invest capital in opening up new land, but even he can get strangled by red tape and prejudice if his plans seem too ambitious. Many Brazilians do realize that their immigration policy has often been unimaginative. After the last war, for example, Brazil might have received a far greater share of displaced persons with skills and qualifications which she could certainly use. But confronted with the restrictions and the attitude of almost instinctive hostility, many of these potential immigrants went elsewhere.

Nevertheless, Brazil did receive a valuable injection of new blood and initiative after 1890; but these immigrants settled mainly in the south and they helped to make the difference between the two Brazils all the more distinct. They were not only Europeans; the Japanese came too, although they only began to arrive in 1910, and they helped to revolutionize farming, market gardening and fisheries. They introduced jute-growing in Amazonia and later began to build industries in São Paulo and Minas. Today, there are almost half a million Japanese in the country and they, too, have settled mostly in the south. By 1920, figures, although very incomplete, showed how unequal the distribution of immigrants has been. While the foreign population of the north was about 46,000, in the south it was 1,225,000. These people were giving birth to a new Brazilian, and although he was outnumbered, and still is, by the product of miscegenation which has been going on for over four hundred years, these new Brazilians were to transform the country; in fact, they created a new Brazil.

By 1930 there were already these two very different types of Brazilians and the new element was not being absorbed by the process of miscegenation. One exception was the Portuguese immigrant. He might have a wife and family back in Portugal, but very soon he acquired what became known as the 'Brazilian wife'. Usually she was Negro and he fathered a second family in Brazil. It was, and to some extent still is, an accepted practice. But during the crucial period of this new immigration, the Portuguese were in a minority and a great many of them were illiterate peasants from the distressed areas of northern Portugal. To this day, the image which Brazilians have of the Portuguese is of a slow-witted, rather comical character whose language, although it is the same as theirs, they now find hard to understand. The Portuguese the Brazilians speak has become softer and with a lilting slowness, which makes it rather like the English of the southern states of America. It has also acquired a new construction and new expressions. In Portugal, and in other parts of South America, it is referred to rudely as *pretogues*, 'black Portuguese'; but the Portuguese also call it, with nostalgia, 'Portuguese with sugar'; for to so many of them Brazil is still a land of promise, gay and free. To the Brazilians, however, even those of Portuguese extraction, Portugal in the sense of mother country means very little now.

Between 1820 and 1933, while the Portuguese accounted for less than 30 per cent of immigration, Italians, Spaniards and Germans accounted for over half; and there were other smaller, but from the point of view of the development of this new Brazil, important contributory streams of immigrants from the former Baltic States and the Near East. Syrians and Lebanese, for example, although there were only about a hundred thousand of them by 1933, made their mark wherever they settled, which again was mainly in the south. Travelling far inland, they became the links between the manu‑facturers and tradesmen in the cities and the consumers in the farming communities and the townships of the interior. Descendants of these immigrants also played a part in building some of Brazil's new industries. The British, the Americans, the French and the Scandinavians came too, but they were not immigrants in the accepted sense of the word. They came to build or to manage factories, railways and public utilities, the insurance and shipping companies, the import and export houses; in fact, to play the same role which they had taken on all over South America, and they brought with them a new code of ethics in business conduct. The expression *palavra de inglês*, 'word of an Englishman', became a colloquialism which is still used to mean word of honour. *Hora inglesa*, 'English time', came to denote punctuality, but that was one innovation which the Brazilian never really adopted. To most of them the function of a clock is to tell the time, not dictate it.

But after 1930 when the Vargas revolution had begun to arouse not only a new social awareness but an even deeper feeling of nationalism, Brazilians began to resent the presence of these foreigners in executive positions. They objected to being subordinate to a foreign head of a department even in a foreign firm, particularly if he had been sent out to do the job. Their reasoning was that if a job was a good one, a Brazilian should have it. It was a case of Brazil for the Brazilians, and this feeling gave rise to legislation which laid down that two‑thirds of the staff of any firm should be Brazilian born. Much the same prejudice against the foreign employer exists in other parts of South America. Yet in Brazil, which prides herself on the success of her experiment in miscegenation and on the fact that in the eyes of her law all men are equal, this discrimination seems to be a little contradictory. The Brazilian explanation is that they are determined to create a society in which all men are treated equally, but it must be a Brazilian society; and in this society the foreigner, whatever his talents, is perhaps rather less equal. It is perhaps a logical reaction of a former colonial people, although their colonial days ended a long time ago. But anxiety to pursue the policy of miscegenation is not by any means as deep as it was. Today there is an entirely new generation which is not the product of mixed races. These new Brazilians, the descendants of the Spaniards, the Germans or the Italians, will not as a rule marry even a mulatto.

What was and still is strong in Brazil is the desire to 'Brazilianize', to ensure that the foreigner should become completely integrated in a Brazilian way of life and thought; and, in the hey-days of national-ism in the 1930s and 1940s, as apparently this could not be achieved by inspiring them to want to be Brazilians, then they must be persuaded to do so by law. After 1930, when Vargas was feverishly fanning this new nationalism, legislation was introduced which obliged exclusively foreign schools and clubs and foreign language newspapers to close. Brazilian nationalists were shocked to discover from the 1940 census that over a million and a half people had actually declared that they did not speak Portuguese in their homes, even though the majority of them were Brazilian born. Although a great many of these new Brazilians have not been fused into what one might call the old Brazilian mould, today within almost every Brazilian, whatever his ancestry may be, there runs the thread of a certain uniformity of outlook and even behaviour which is uniquely Brazilian. What is more remarkable is that this uniformity and some of these distinctive traits have taken root so quickly. But it has been due less to nationalistic legislation than to pride in their own achieve-ments, and as far as the new Brazilians are concerned, miscegenation had nothing to do with it.

Many Brazilian historians have made almost a mystique of mis-cegenation and a newcomer to Brazilian affairs may sometimes be given the impression that it was a calculated experiment in socio-logical policy. It was nothing of the sort. It was partly the result of chance, but mainly through necessity. For well over three hundred years after her discovery, white women were scarce in Brazil and the early Portuguese settlers turned first to the Indian women and later to their African slaves for solace. While other European colonizers in Africa tended to resist intimacy with the Negro, the Portuguese never had any such inhibitions, and it was the same in Brazil. Gilberto Freyre, one of Brazil's most distinguished sociologists, advances a theory that the Iberian people, after their conquest by the Moors, not unnaturally came to regard the dark-skinned race which was to be their master for so long as a superior people, which in fact they were. Hence it was not only a lack of prejudice in the Portuguese which led them to mate freely with the black or brown woman, but an almost instinctive respect for colour. It may also explain why the Portuguese in Brazil treated their slaves as well as they did; and in more recent times the Portuguese are admittedly almost the only immigrants who do not hesitate to marry the Negro and so carry on the process of miscegenation. But whatever the reasons, it has cer-tainly been a success. It has ensured that the great negroid element in the country, however wretched their existence may have become in other ways since the abolition of slavery, was never made to feel positively inferior; and so it has not become, at least so far, a sullen, vindictive element. A great many Brazilians maintain that miscegena-tion has created in Brazil a unique society in which the perils of racial discrimination have been eliminated. They will also furiously refute arguments that it may have led to a certain degeneration. But do all Brazilians today feel the same?

Brazil is often held up as a shining example of a nation which has solved her racial problem. She has done no such thing, for the simple reason that the problem has never arisen. It is likely that it never will, yet even in Brazil there are the ingredients of possible racial tensions in the future, although it is perhaps misleading, because of the implications, to refer to such tensions as racial. They are more likely to be part of a much broader conflict, the revolt, which has already begun, of that majority of Brazilians who live in a world apart, a world lacking in opportunity and social justice. The Negro has always been the predominant element in this world of the have-nots, and it is a status which he so far seems to accept in the same philosophical way as he accepts what one might venture to call the discrimination with a smile which he does experience now.

There is an awareness of colour in Brazil, and to a far greater degree than is often realized by some sociologists who applaud the success of Brazilian racial tolerance but who have never seen it at close quarters. Certainly there is no harsh prejudice, nothing even remotely resembling the attitude to colour of the South Africans or the North Americans. But the distinction is made. Some Brazilians will still argue that the white element in the country retains its social superiority not because of race but only thanks to education and financial status; and in effect this is true, and it applies not only in the distinction between the white and the coloured man. Financial status commands almost reverence among the new Brazilian upper and middle classes, but nearly all Brazilians seem to have acquired the New World tendency to judge a man by the size of his bank account.

The fact remains that racial discrimination does exist, although the Brazilians are infinitely generous in their definition of white. In South Africa 'white' Brazilians have been shocked to find themselves being told blandly by hotel receptionists that there has been some mistake over their reservations. But in Brazil itself, even Negro diplomats and artists have, on occasion, been refused rooms in first-class hotels; and although many Brazilians will assure you that discrimination is something which never even enters their minds, in the 1950s it was felt necessary to introduce legislation making racial discrimination an offence. In the eyes of the law a Negro has precisely the same rights as any white man, and socially a poor Negro and a poor white are on the same footing; it is only when the former attempts to advance that he comes up against the barriers. Yet this discrimination, this economic segregation, is still very largely a tacit one. A Negro will tell you without any apparent rancour that in a good hotel or shop the only job he can get is behind the scenes; in the kitchens, or in the packing department. Certainly you will not often see a Negro or even a dark half-caste in any position of real responsibility. This gentle discrimination exists to a far greater extent in the south, but you will also find it in Rio which is still very much in the negroid coastal belt which stretches down from the north.

What precisely is the proportion of negroids in the population today is difficult to say. There is a shyness about colour which makes statistics somewhat unrealistic, for the number of Brazilians who declare themselves to be white seems to be out of proportion to the figures for immigration and the population increase generally, quite apart from the evidence of one's eyes. The census authorities admit that persons claiming to be white would not be regarded as such in other countries. In the 1940 census, for example, out of a population of just over 41,000,000, 'Negroes' accounted for approximately 6,000,000, but only about another 8,700,000 declared themselves to be other than 'white'. In 1950 the population had increased to almost 52,000,000, of which 5,700,000 were 'Negroes' while fewer than 13,800,000 described themselves as in any way coloured.

This feeling about colour makes Brazilians, even those who are not exactly white, feel offended when they hear Brazil being described, particularly by other South Americans, as a coloured country. They will assure you that this is not due to any shame at their ethnical background. In the Brazilian mind, Negro and colour have become synonomous with backwardness and inferiority; and so a coloured Brazilian who does climb the social ladder considers he has earned the right to call himself white. Even the English expression 'native born' when applied to a Brazilian is regarded as derogatory. This touchiness can even extend to the sort of clothes a European may wear. When President Janio Quadros, part of whose tremendous appeal was his informality, began to appear in public wearing a bush shirt, Brazilians muttered to each other: 'Where does he think he is, Africa?'

The real problem is that while the white population and the economy of the south expand, a way of life is being created which already has a tempo of activity and disciplines which are foreign and even distasteful to the temperament of the Negro and of the more easygoing Brazilian of mixed blood of the north. Some Brazilians will argue that the Negro, in particular, does not aspire to this sort of life, but they add that, even if he did, he would not have the educational qualifications to compete. According to these Brazilians, a great many people who live in this other world of hovels and shanty towns do so from choice because they lack ambition and are content in their freedom from the rules and the shove and push of the world or progress around them. There is a good deal of truth in this too, although this lack of initiative is also due to debilitating endemic diseases and malnutrition, which for a very great many of these Brazilians have become inescapable facts of life. Certainly, in almost any institution, from parliament to even the junior ranks of the officer class in the armed forces, the Negro, and to a great extent the dark mulatto, are conspicuous by their absence. But one cannot help wondering what might happen when the opportunities for education and a healthier life became very much greater and a new generation of Negroes too can acquire the qualifications and the energy to compete for a place in the new society which Brazilian reformers, despite the negative attitude of traditional conservative classes, are still trying to build after the social upheaval wrought by the Vargas era.

One of their hardest tasks will be to prevent the already wide gap between the two Brazils, the great dark north and the relatively small white south, becoming even wider. A greater tragedy, perhaps, could be if the negroid population, multiplying and concentrated in the north and conditioned by environment, and by their almost voluntary segregation, are not inspired to change their attitude to life. The poverty in the future of a great many of these Brazilians may not be related to unemployment, but to their increasing unemployability in an expanding but more exacting society.

Foreign writers who have weighed the potentialities and the prob-lems of Brazil can often reach widely conflicting conclusions.[7] Most of them, like Stefan Zweig, who called Brazil 'The Land of the Future', see in this vast country of opportunities still only partially explored, a great new potential power in a modern world. Others come to a very different and depressing verdict, although it is not necessarily always a realistic one. Anyone who has seen what the Brazilians can achieve, despite often tremendous obstacles, can have few doubts about the brightness of Brazil's future in a changing world, even though it may still be some way off. Conventional economists, however, are appalled by her economic acrobatics, while some sociologists can see in Brazil all the right conditions for almost any kind of social upheaval and political extremism.

To some extent, both are right. When the economists predict that Brazil could become a huge economic slum they are correct in so far that this could certainly happen to parts of Brazil; some of them already are human slums. As regards possible social disaster and extremism, one can only rely on the reassuring evidence of history and the Brazilian temperament as safeguards against that. This may not be so in the future when the social awareness of the masses is fully awakened. Yet Brazil has weathered some frightening crises even in recent times. There was the advent and the downfall of Vargas, not once, but twice; another was the overthrow of the left-wing government of President Goulart who claimed to carry Vargas's torch, and the almost forcible steering of the country back to the Right as recently as 1964. In many other countries, and not necessarily only in Latin America, such crises might not have been overcome quite so peacefully.

When one looks at the dark side of Brazil one can often be distracted from appreciating the infinitely brighter other side, just as the memory of the matted green wilderness of central Brazil can be so haunting long after one is back in the blaring civilization of a city. What is almost more disturbing to anyone who has come to know Brazil intimately is not what may happen in the future but what is happening now. It is the contrasts of Brazil, and essentially the contrasts in the life and in the attitude of people, which are so disturbing. The encouraging thing is that today many more Brazilians, not only of the growing middle class but of that strata who once contemplated the poverty all around them with almost the same detachment as a man in a London pub might discuss an epidemic of influenza in the Hebrides, are becoming distressed and conscience-stricken too by the spectacle of poverty. Working conditions and welfare facilities in many of the larger firms and industries, and even on some of those great farms in São Paulo and Minas and in the far south, are as advanced now as any in the world. But although there are also government social welfare schemes and a very great measure of protection of labour in the towns, the lower-income Brazilian is still a very defenceless person in many ways. This class of Brazilian can still find himself in deep trouble if illness, for instance, should strike his family. Pensions and sickness allowances are far from adequate and sometimes difficult to claim and collect. The plight of the rural population is infinitely worse, in fact a great many of these Brazilians, even those of the not so remote interior, live outside the economy of the country. But at a conservative esti-mate, based on official figures for incomes, half of Brazil's population of seventy-nine million exist at a very low level indeed;[8] and a great many of these Brazilians live in towns surrounded by all the trappings of progress and prosperity.

It can be argued that such statistics are misleading because even the Brazilian whose income is the equivalent of only a few shillings a day is better off than many inhabitants of other underdeveloped parts of the world; of those bleak and barren distressed areas, for example, of the Andean countries. The cold reassurance of the foot-notes to these statistics is that the Brazilian needs few clothes, he has no problem of heating, and in the interior, and even in the shanty encampments on the outskirts of the towns, he can produce most of his food. But the fact remains that while parts of Brazil, and many of the people who live in them, are enjoying a degree of prosperity which is higher than almost anywhere else in Latin America, almost forty million other Brazilians live in conditions which are among the lowest. But it is not just a matter of economic neediness. Poverty in Brazil is a very relative term. The average income of a man in the northeast, for example, is less than £35 ($98) a year. In the state of São Paulo he could earn five times that. He might earn even more as a domestic servant in Rio. As a skilled factory worker he could take home a wage which, allowing for the difference in cost of living but, above all, in his requirements, would give him a standard of life comparable to that of a worker in industry in Europe.

The poverty of so many of these needy millions is measured not in terms of cash but in mental and physical capacity. To lapse into the clinical language of statistics, so many of these Brazilians are un-productive elements of society because their energy, or any individual ambitions they might have, are sapped by disease. Malnutrition is only a consequence of this chronic state of debility. In the interior, and even in rural surroundings on the outskirts of the towns, you will find families and whole communities who grow only the barest essentials for their existence because they often lack the physical strength to clear the ground around them. Among these people, parasitic and tropical diseases have taken root and tuberculosis is still one of the greatest killers. The Brazilian has one of the lowest expectations of life in Latin America. The national average is forty-three years, although in the more developed areas it is nearing sixty. In many parts of the country, however, and particularly in the north, it is less than forty years. This is why a newcomer to Brazil is often struck by the fact that he rarely sees old people about. Brazil is a country of the young. In the 1950 census, out of every thousand persons only twenty-four were found to be sixty-five years old or more.

Brazil also has one of the highest birth-rates in the world, almost fifty for every thousand inhabitants. Each year, over two million babies are born alive, but infant mortality is also one of the highest in the world. Of every thousand babies, 170 will die in their first year. But that is the national average. In the south it is between 86 and 97; in certain parts of the north it is as high as 243. These high rates of births and deaths, however, are not so much confined to areas as to classes and, above all, ethnic groups. The registered birth-rate, for example, among the negroid population is almost 200 for every thousand, whereas the national average is about 44. But in the interior, in particular, a great many births are not officially registered. Despite the incidence of disease and higher mortality, this negroid and under-privileged element is still increasing at a faster rate than the more socially advanced Brazilians.

The fight against this poverty has become the avowed crusade of every government since Vargas made concern for the under-privileged a political issue, as well as one of conscience. After 1945 the presidential term of office, which had been four years, was extended to five, and every successive president has had his own five-year plan to raise standards of living. The poorer Brazilian may show a remarkable, almost saintly patience; but not the politician or the reformer. Many of these plans and the great development programmes which have been launched were sincere and meticulous in detail and they all faced squarely the problem of poverty, the lack of transport and irrigation, and all the other consequences of under-development. But so many of them, even those plans which were spread out over much longer periods, were unrealistic in so far as they were too ambitious for Brazil's resources. Brasilia is the sort of example of this impatience for progress which appals the economists. Even a highly developed country might have considered twenty-five, or even forty years a practical period in which to build a new capital and uproot the machinery of government. Brazil planned to do it all in five years. Imaginative as the plan was, to create a new focus of progress in the interior, the devastating cost to the country's economy is still difficult to assess.

Some Brazilian politicians and reformers counter the charge that economically their plans are often wildly unorthodox with the argu-ment that Brazil's problem of underdevelopment is so great, and her need to improve the lot of so many people is so imperative, that they call for unconventional solutions. President Kubitscheck in 1956 summed up the feelings of many Brazilians with his slogan 'Fifty years progress in five', and a policy which was virtually to 'build now and pay later'. During his five-year term of office he certainly built a great deal, but by July 1964 Brazil owed the world the equivalent of $3,400,000,000, rather more than £1,220,000,000, which was higher than the entire gold and convertible currency reserves of the United Kingdom in July of that same year.

Brazilians, however, are not unduly perturbed by these debts. They are confident of their ability to pay them, eventually. They also feel that the foreigners who lend them money or give them credits to enable them to carry on importing are prompted by three basic reasons. The Americans, they claim, do so because they fear that unless Brazil can raise the standards of living of the masses she might become an easy prize for the communists and the disciples of Fidel

127

Castro. Others, including the Americans, extend credits, not out of charity but also from purely business motives. Thirdly, they are sure that any far-sighted foreigner must realize what a tremendous new field for enterprise Brazil could be, and where, furthermore, he will not find that pyschological hostility which exists in Africa and Asia. In Brazilian minds, all that these foreigners are doing, and very sensibly, is to invest in their future.

Brazilians' over-spending, based on this confidence, has been almost a calculated policy at times; and they argue that, thanks to it, they have achieved a far greater degree of progress, and far more quickly, than they would have done if they had followed the ortho-dox rules of economics. It may all sound positively blasphemous to the conventional, and what has gone seriously wrong is that today, as a result of her patchy development and also due to the fact that while the world price of her exports has been falling, the cost of the goods and raw materials which she must import has risen, a statistical picture of Brazil's economy is etched in deep, and apparently in-delible, red. Brazil is in the position now of a man who, in his anxiety to provide his family with all the benefits, and the gadgetry, of the twentieth century, finds himself entangled in the meshes of the finance companies. But the simile is a bad one, for despite Brazil's anguish for progress, whatever the cost, there are still those millions in the growing Brazilian family who have benefited very little, if at all.

The attitude to the continued material and spiritual poverty of so many people seems almost comparable to the attitude of earlier Brazilians to the problem of slavery. But today there is a public opinion with an infinitely greater influence than existed in the days when the abolitionists launched their crusade. Surely, if Brazilians felt strongly enough about the plight of such a large proportion of their own people, they could force governments to act? That question implies a certain heartlessness in the Brazilian nature which, in fact, does not exist. Basically he is a sentimental and kindly person. He reflects the warmth of the ordinary people of the Iberian peninsula and the Mediterranean, the level-headedness of the solid German and the qualities of immigrants of other nationalities who are in many cases his very recent ancestors. But the new Brazilians, particularly in the south, enjoying a prosperity which they have worked very hard to build, do perhaps have a tendency to be impatient with the apparent fecklessness of the older and poorer Brazilian, not only in the distant north but in their own midst. In the past, when there have been proposals to lay foundations of possibly new industrial centres in some more backward parts of the country, the Paulista, for example, does not always hide his feeling that such expenditure is a gamble. Why, he asks, should not more money be spent on expanding an industrial machine which already exists and which has proved its efficiency from the point of view of the human element too?

There is also another class of Brazilians, although they are slowly changing their attitude, who are all for reforms, providing they do not encroach on their traditional preserves. How, for instance, can agrarian reform be carried out, and the growing problem of the landless peasant still living in almost feudal conditions, be faced realistically in a country where a great proportion of the land is owned by a handful of landlords? Over 62 per cent of agricultural holdings, with an area of 1,300 acres or more, is in the hands of fewer than 3½ per cent of the country's landowners. A great proportion of many of these huge farms is not cultivated; large areas are used only as pasture and such farming as exists on these estates is often done by tenant farmers or share-croppers who have so little security of tenure that they are not inspired to improve their holdings.

Many other great landowners prefer to produce exportable crops such as coffee rather than food for the home market. It is far more profitable, thanks to the policy of successive governments to guarantee the coffee growers an outlet even in times of surplus. In years when Brazil produces more coffee than she can sell, the government will buy up unexportable coffee and so great sums have become immobilized in accumulating stocks of coffee which nobody wants. The smaller landowners are often far more progressive than the traditional land barons who stubbornly resist change. But many of these smaller farms are not large enough to be worked economically by modern methods. Another factor in Brazil's still primitive agricultural scene is not only the poor health of the farm worker but his illiteracy and often shocking backwardness even, to some extent, in the more advanced states of the south. One result of all this is that Brazil must import food. Another is that the rural community is the great reservoir of those dispirited, forgotten Brazilians, so many of whom drift away to seek a new but dubious security in and around the towns.

Agrarian reform in Brazil does not mean simply breaking up the great estates, and the amalgamation of the smaller, uneconomic farms in the way the Japanese, for example, have done so successfully in São Paulo with their co-operatives. This would be hard enough, but it also means such a radical revision of attitude, so many reforms particularly of health and educational services, and the slaughter of so many sacred cows – the democratization of King Coffee, for example – that it is not surprising that so many governments, even the Vargas régime, have baulked at the prospect, and the political consequences. For a politician to talk too fervently of agrarian reform is a sure way of getting himself stamped as a communist or, what is perhaps even worse, a communist tool. President Goulart had intro-duced an agrarian reform Bill just before he was deposed. His solution was admittedly drastic and not too carefully considered, but it was his last act as president; the final evidence, that his régime had swung too far to the left. In some ways, agrarian reform, too, has become similar to the issue of slavery. Almost all Brazilians who think about it agree that it must be carried out, not only for the sake of the country's economy but as a matter of conscience. The Church urges it and it was one of the first measures proposed by the right-wing caretaker government which took over in April of 1964. The reform it proposed, however, would be carried out at a more rational pace, calling for progressively higher taxes on idle land and provid-ing for greater compensation to landowners in cases of expropriation.

Another of those glaring contradictions, for a country which worships progress, is the Brazilian attitude to education and parti-cularly illiteracy. But, like poverty, illiteracy is confined to a class and an ethnic group towards which many Brazilians feel a certain impatience, rather than outright indifference, although at times it seems like it. Seventy-five years ago, at the time of the fall of the

Empire, something like 90 per cent of the population, then about 14 million, was illiterate. Today, there are 79 million Brazilians of which half are illiterate. But literacy is as relative a term as poverty. Many Brazilians who claim to be able to read and write can do little more than laboriously spell out words and draw, rather than sign their name. Like poverty, the seeds of illiteracy were sown a long time ago. Throughout colonial days and during the period of the Empire and of the first republic, education for the ordinary Brazilian was almost an unobtainable commodity. The right to free education was written into the Constitution of 1934; but Brazil's educational system is still the despair of those reformers who appreciate more than ever what illiteracy alone is costing the country.

For almost four hundred years education in Brazil had been the privilege of the rich; and although this might suggest that the ruling classes had founded universities for their own youth, as they did in Spanish America, this was not so. The Brazilian university is a very new institution. The first was opened in Rio only in 1920; but until then there had been only two universities in the whole of the Portuguese-speaking world: the Universities of Coimbra and Lisbon. It would seem that the Brazilians inherited another Portuguese characteristic, that suspicion of education, particularly for the masses, which the ruling classes in Portugal still have. This was true in Brazil's early days after independence, in fact it was true for a very long time afterwards. It is not so today, although the new regard for education might seem to exist more in principle than in fact. For the lower-paid Brazilian, even elementary education is still a commodity in short supply. Higher education is almost entirely beyond his means. In rural areas the picture is far more dismal. At an overall average, less than a quarter of Brazilians over the age of fifteen who live in the towns cannot read or write; in rural areas about 70 per cent are illiterate and in the northeast the percentage is still almost as high as it was seventy-five years ago when the Empire fell.

The paucity of public funds available for education would seem to indicate a still deep-rooted indifference, although this does not apply in southern Brazil where private enterprise has co-operated in the fight against illiteracy much more than it has done in other parts of the country. In 1946 education became the joint responsibility of the Federal, state and municipal governments. But the actual sums for education set aside each year have been a very small fraction of the national income. As the population grows, so does the number of illiterates, for there are not enough schools or teachers to cope with this increase. In the southern states it is calculated that fewer than 5 per cent of children have no schools to go to; but in the northeast it is near to 56 per cent. The Brazilian authorities admit that only about a tenth of adolescents attend school and out of every hundred of these, only seven complete their schooling. This mass truancy, encouraged by parents, is another of the problems which face the authorities, particularly in the north and in most rural areas. To the mentality of the Brazilians of these parts of the country, a mentality which has been bred by long neglect and by the deadening environment of poverty in so many forms, schooling, even if it exists, seems to be merely a waste of an extra pair of hands which can help to contribute to the meagre family income. This is the sort of attitude which prompts certain Brazilians to argue that many of their countrymen who live in that other Brazil of hovels and squalor do so from choice; it is one more of those disconcerting facets of the Brazilian character.

In a country where half the population is in its teens, this neglect of education in its broader aspects and the lack of interest or even faith in schooling which the poorer Brazilian often shows is the despair of the reformers. This high proportion of young people is quoted many times as a reason why an allout campaign to provide even a basic education for Brazil's growing millions, even if they all wanted it, is beyond the country's means at the moment. It is a fact which some Brazilians also use to justify a concentration now of Brazil's limited resources on higher and technical education. This, they argue, will ensure a greater supply of skilled men and planners which Brazil needs badly to build up industry and a new and progressive society which in time would absorb these great pockets of poverty and lassitude. But the facts do not seem to bear out the theory.

Admittedly there has been a marked development in higher and technical education generally. Since 1920 twentyfour universities have been founded and another five are in the process of formation. But of these, eighteen are in the south, eleven of them in the three states of São Paulo, Rio and Minas Gerais which also account for a great proportion of the technical and other schools in the country. This concentration in the south also of privately owned or endowed schools and universities is only to be expected. But the policy of expanding higher education as part of a broader development plan appears to have a distinctly regional and class basis. The upper classes and the new economic *élite*, particularly in the south, seem more concerned with providing the kind of education which their own children and potential employees will need in order to carry on the society they have created, rather than with the national problem of illiteracy. They have seen to it that it is no longer such a problem in their part of Brazil; São Paulo, for example, has spent almost as much on education as all the other Brazilian states together.

Until such time as there is a co-ordinated and far more generously conceived and financed educational programme on a national basis, illiteracy will continue to be another factor which divides Brazil in two. Even Vargas, with all his proclaimed solicitude for the lower classes, could not do very much about it either. Although it is claimed that during the fifteen years of his first régime illiteracy dropped by ten per cent, in view of the natural population growth during that time the actual number of illiterates increased.

The continued neglect of this problem, apart from its economic consequences – the primitiveness of so much of Brazil's agriculture, for example – is creating a people apart. And it prompts a theory that it is a calculated policy of one classs of Brazilian to keep the voices of the majority, if not hushed entirely, at least controlled. Every Brazilian over the age of eighteen is entitled to vote. In fact, he is not only entitled, he is obliged by law to exercise his right, and he is fined if he does not. But he must be literate. As half of Brazil's population is under the age of eighteen, this would allow for an electorate of over 40 million. But the electorate today is not quite 19 million; and, as every literate adult Brazilian is strictly obliged by law to register as a voter (in fact, his voting papers are virtually his legal identity card) it is evident that more than 20 million Brazilians –

over half the adult population – are disenfranchised on the grounds of illiteracy. This essential qualification which a voter must have has also meant a disproportionate concentration of political influence in the south. The state of São Paulo alone, for example, accounts for about a quarter of the electorate of the entire country, although the Paulistas represent less than 19 per cent of Brazil's population.

These voiceless Brazilians constitute an element that has the most to complain about. They are the Negroes, the coloured population of the north and the forgotten people of the interior; the landless peasants and those stricken inhabitants of the Sertões of the northeast nursing their dry earth. Even the Brazilians of this strata who belong to trade unions can have their voices muffled. Trade unionism in the accepted sense does not exist. Labour is organized into workers' syndicates which are controlled by the government; and although the right to strike, for example, is recognized, it is so conditional that the government can intervene at any time. These syndicates, with an often large membership of workers from rural areas, have had little experience of true trade-union procedures or collective bargaining; and they must often rely entirely on the government to decree new wage minimums and working conditions. The syndicates are there-fore very much a political instrument in which the bulk of their membership is naïve and has very little say. They are consequently also wide open to infiltration by communists and other agitators, or just axe-grinders. The person responsible for this system was Vargas. He saw in the disorganization of labour, particularly in the growing industries, an opportunity not only of giving these new and increas-ingly important workers a status, but also of creating a new support for himself. The elaborate labour code which he introduced in 1943 has been basically maintained by subsequent governments and as a result what in any liberal country are considered to be the prerogatives of trade unions, in Brazil are exercised by the government.

It is perhaps true that the economic *élite* may see a measure of safety in the enforced silence of the under-privileged merely because of their inability to read and write. It would be unfair to say, how-ever, that many of the *élite*, and middle-class Brazilians, too, in their comparatively cosy prosperity, are not ashamed of this deep-rooted poverty in their midst of which illiteracy is only one consequence. But Brazilians seem to have become conditioned to the sight of poverty, which has become a feature of the Brazilian scenery. A rich Brazilian – and his wealth and way of life can often stand up to any international standard of opulence – can look out of his window on to a maze of hovels on a hillside or at the end of the street, in which there is no running water, no drains, and where people are visibly underfed. One of his middle-class employees may live farther down the same street, in a far more modest flat, of course, but he, too, can look out through the nylon curtains on to this other Brazil on his doorstep. The sight of those pathetic funeral processions, with bobbing children carrying the small white coffin, may no longer remind him of the melancholy statistics of which they are the evidence; he has seen such processions so often. Even the sensitiveness of the newly arrived foreigner can very soon become dulled by the repetitiveness of the picture of poverty in its many forms.

Brazil has experienced many revolutions, and so far they have come about in a singularly placid manner. Yet the greatest revolution, the biggest reform of all, is still to come, and it can only be hoped that the more fortunate Brazilians will start it. The great day will be when these Brazilians, proud, and justly so, of their achievements, look out of their windows and really see how very big the other Brazil is becoming.

46 This vaqueiro or cowboy is a typical figure of northeastern Brazil.

47 This family of the northeast lives in relatively good conditions compared with the gruelling poverty of most of this region.

48 In southern Brazil German influence is still very evident. This is the office of a German language newspaper in Blumenau.

49 Two main racial types in Brazil are Indian and Negro. This coastal family of Indian descent has a Negro nursemaid.

50 Many of the Indians of the interior are still very primitive. An early photograph of an Indian of Central Brazil.

51 An Indian family of the interior.

52 Brazil is predominantly Roman Catholic. These votive offerings represent stricken or diseased human limbs and are to be found on the altars of shrine churches.

53 Christianity and voodoo worship (macumba) co-exist. This is a macumba ceremony in a *terreiro* or place of worship.

54 Another feature of macumba is the fetish cult of *Omulu* with its mysterious rituals.

55 Many Brazilians will dutifully attend Mass on Sunday but just as dutifully visit a terreiro during the week. A church procession in Ouro Prêto.

56 These Indians of the interior still use traditional primitive methods of 'curing' the sick.

57 This class of women of mixed races is being taught child care.

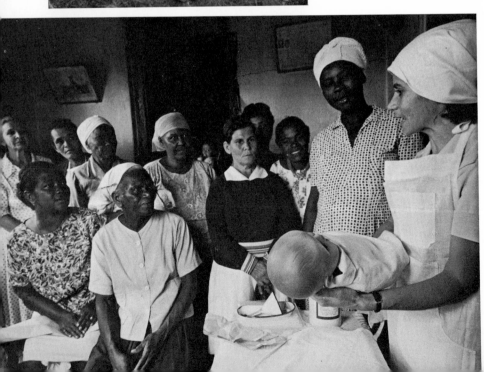

58 The right to free education is contained in the Brazilian Constitution. This state secondary school is in the steel town of Volta Redonda.

59 These children are being taught at a state primary school. But there are not enough schools and teachers to cope with the population increase and consequent high illiteracy rate.

60 A typical street market at Penedo in Alagôas.

61 The Indian crafts of the interior are being encouraged as a tourist attraction.

9   The Faces of Culture

ANYONE SEEKING TO UNDERSTAND the Brazilians by trying
to trace the origins and development of their culture would find
scanty, though intriguing, material to work on if he started his
researches much before the nineteenth century. In the early sixteenth
century, when the first Portuguese began to arrive, they found no
indigenous civilization, no established culture such as the Spaniards
had discovered among the Chibcha people of Colombia or the
Myas of the Yucatan and Guatemala and in the elaborate civilizations of the Aztecs and of the Inca Empire which spread from
Ecuador, through Peru and Bolivia, down to Chile. Although the
Spanish conquerors, in their Christian crusade to the New World
and in the greed aroused by the unexpected sight of the treasure
which the heathens had amassed, destroyed these civilizations, their
culture lived on to inspire early Spanish-American artists and
writers. It is still vividly evident in the themes of such men as the
Mexican Diogo Rivera and in the visual art and in the writings of
other twentieth-century Latin Americans of mixed Spanish and
Indian descent. At the time Cervantes was creating Don Quixote,
the half-Indian Peruvian, Garcilaso de la Vega, was writing the
history of Peru, *Commentarios Reales, que tratan del origen de los Yincas*.
Brazil's cultural history can record no equivalent figure.

The early Portuguese settlers and those who followed them during
the next three centuries were, to put it kindly, far from culturally
inclined. Portuguese masons and wood carvers came to build the
great churches of Bahia and later those of Rio and Minas Gerais, but
little else. There was virtually no other form of art, and certainly
nothing which might be termed Brazilian art, until the appearance

of the mulatto Antonio Francisco in the eighteenth century. He became known, for tragic reasons, as *Aleijadinho*, the little cripple, and his sculptures and carvings for the churches of Ouro Prêto are the first expression of Brazilian art of any significance. The religious orders and, above all, the Jesuits who arrived in 1549 devoted most of their efforts to converting the Indians and to the hopeless battle of protecting them from slavery. Although they founded the only schools in the colony, they neither brought with them, nor did they ever show, during the two hundred years they remained in Brazil, any inspiring interest in the arts outside the Church.

The first taste of culture was given to Brazil not by a Portuguese but by a Dutchman in the seventeenth century, almost a hundred and forty years after Brazil's discovery. The Dutch had established a settlement in Pernambuco and Maurice of Nassau brought in architects, painters and scholars but they left no following behind them when in 1654 the Dutch were driven out. The French, who had also held part of Brazil, but for a very brief period, in that same century, left virtually no traces. Brazil, in fact, was isolated by the Portuguese from the rest of the world, both materially and in spirit – and as a calculated policy – until 1808. In that year Dom João, the Prince Regent, and the Portuguese court took refuge in Brazil from the Napoleonic War. Until then, the Church had been the only outlet for such artistic expression as there was. Now, the Court was to provide another patronage and of a different kind.

In 1816 Dom João brought a French artistic mission to Brazil. It was led by Joachim Lebreton, the Secretary of the École des Beaux Arts in Paris, and it included sculptors and painters, among them Debret, Taunay and the brothers Ferrez. But, as Dr Celso Kelly, Professor of the History of Art at the University of Brazil, was to point out almost one hundred and fifty years later, the group could hardly be said to have represented the best that France could boast of in the way of artists. Certainly it did not include any adventurous spirits. The mission imposed a rigidly academic standard, a frigid discipline of draftsmanship which Brazilian painters in particular imitated, although it was foreign to their nature and inhibited them from finding expression more suited to their temperament. Debret's work in Brazil was concerned with consolidating the influence of the newly formed Imperial Academy of Fine Arts and the dictates of the Court *Salon*. The rigidity these imposed, and their insistence on an academic treatment of historical subjects and portraiture as comprising the proper field of artistic endeavour, struck no deep chord in the Brazilian artist. The only exponents of any note of this school of painting were Pedro Américo de Figueiredo and Vítor Meirelles. Debret, however, found one Brazilian to carry on this attempt to implant an alien tradition: Araujo Porto Alegre. The result of this imposing of a mask, rather than the fashioning of a face of culture, was to check for a long time a natural evolution of Brazilian painting.

It was only after the proclamation of the Republic in 1889 that Brazilian artists became less inhibited and began to paint what they saw around them. One of the first of these was Almeida Junior, a painter of the backlands and of the northeast. He was awarded a scholarship to Paris but, as some Brazilian art historians noted, he 'did not allow himself to be seduced by the technical innovations he found there'; and he returned apparently uninfluenced by the impres/ sionist, or any other movement. Other Brazilians, in their anxiety to 'nationalize' their art, were to react in the same way for years to come. It would have seemed that the cubists and the surrealists, for example, in their break with tradition, would have aroused a response among the Brazilians. Yet the new movements were a long time in coming to Brazil. In fact, aesthetic unrest did not begin to stir until after the First World War, and only then did it succeed in finally freeing Brazilian artists from the academic tendency that had dominated them. In spite of Dom João's enthusiastic and well/meaning en/ couragement, particularly of painting which was to be the favourite of the arts for many years, it was over a century before anything which could be called a Brazilian school of painting emerged.

The influence of modern movements, when it came, released in the Brazilian painter that deep feeling of nationalism which has been the strength and the inspiration of the country's more notable writers too. Cândido Portinari, who achieved an international reputation, is perhaps the one outstanding example. Dr Celso Kelly says of him:

147

He made a study of the purple-red earth of his native São Paulo; he took a stand on practical subjects; he caught the lyric note in the Brazilian landscape and the soul of the people; he worked on plebeian themes and constructed the human figure in the realism of squalor and ugliness. There is something *American* about him in his points of resemblance with the Mexicans, Diego Rivera and José Clemente Orozco.

Since the end of the Second World War, the New Brazilians of the south have begun opening new windows for the Brazilian artist too. In São Paulo the Museum of Modern Art, largely privately endowed, today houses one of the finest collections outside Europe and the United States. It was Paulistas' enterprise, also, that gave their city a claim to recognition in the world of art with its Biennial Exhibition of Modern Art, an event which, perhaps more than any other, has established contact between the Brazilian artist and new movements.

The slowness of the emergence of artistic expression of any consequence, even in painting which had been so encouraged, is all the more striking, if not surprising, in Brazilian literature. Stefan Zweig, in his often eulogistic study *Brazil, Land of the Future*, published in 1942, wrote in praise of contemporary culture:

In order properly to appreciate this specific accomplishment, one must not forget that the whole intellectual life of this nation is hardly more than one hundred years old, and that in the preceding three hundred colonial years, every form of cultural development had been systematically suppressed.

Just as Brazilians in the nineteenth century had suggested bitterly that books on Portuguese colonization of Brazil should be classified under fiction in the solitary public library at the time, Brazilians today still look back at their cultural history with resentment at that intellectual vacuum which the Portuguese created and maintained for as long as they could.

The isolation of Brazil was prompted by Portugal's determination to retain for herself the monopoly of trade, if such it could be called, and of any wealth which the colony had to offer. In the context of the times, and in view of the rivalries which this small Iberian country of limited resources had to face, it was perhaps an under, standable policy. But the Portuguese went further. The poverty, not only of culture but of even basic education as late as the nineteenth century, was not due only to the intellectual backwardness of so many of the Portuguese settlers who came to Brazil; it was also part of a calculated policy.

When in time the settlers began to demand something better in the way of education than the restricted facilities, in more senses than one, which the Church provided, their demands were rejected. A request by the colonists in Minas Gerais, for example, to set up a medical school which they were prepared to finance themselves was turned down on the grounds that graduates of the Portuguese Empire should all pass through one university in Portugal: Coimbra. It was a policy aimed not merely at centralizing higher education, but of unifying and fashioning a Portuguese outlook in all subjects of the Empire; and it is a policy which basically the Portuguese still pursue in their overseas possessions today, particularly in the great African territories of Angola and Mozambique. This was some, thing which the Spaniards never resorted to, at least not to the same extent, and its effects in Brazil seem to have lingered for a long time. While in the former Spanish colonies of South America some twenty universities had already been established by the nineteenth century, Brazil's first university was only founded in 1920, thirty,one years after her independence.

But there was also a lack of concern for education generally as is realized when one considers the high illiteracy rate at the time of the fall of the Empire and even today. Some Brazilians, however, do not blame the intellectual suppression of the past as much as one might expect for the slowness of the development of their culture, parti, cularly in literature. What happened to the Brazilian painters also happened to the writers, as Gilberto Freyre explains:

For a long time, Brazilian art and literature remained almost inarticulate and passively colonial or sub,European. Aleijadinho,

149

the mulatto sculptor, was one of the few artists to appear with a socially significant artistic message and a technique distinguished by creativeness, audacity and non-European characteristics in a century marked, in Brazil, by academic literature and imitative art.[9]

As Gilberto Freyre says, the inarticulateness of the Brazilians was to last for a very long time and it was poetry which was to become a vehicle of expression long before the novel. In fact, it was only in the second half of the nineteenth century that the truly Brazilian writer began to appear. It was undoubtedly the poets of Minas Gerais of the late eighteenth century, although it was some time before they, too, were able to cut loose from Portuguese influence and imitativeness, who laid the foundations of Brazilian letters. One of the best known of these was José Basilio da Gama whose work, particularly his poem, O Uruguay, in 1769, has survived as a classic example of the trends of that time. After 1830, Brazilian poets were to become deeply influenced by French romanticism, but this period also produced Antonio Gonçalves Dias (1823–64) whom Samuel Putnam acclaims as Brazil's greatest poet,[10] and in whose work, Poesias Americanas, Putnam saw a combining of the spirits of the Indian, the Negro and the Portuguese. Another of the poets who was to achieve distinction was Castro Alves (1847–71). He devoted his poetic eloquence to the cause of the abolition of slavery and became known ever after as the 'poet of the slaves'.

Once the Brazilian poets and particularly the writers found their feet on the familiar and fertile ground of their homeland, literary development has been such that today Brazil has usurped Portugal as the centre of new thought and writing in the Portuguese-speaking world. The work of Machado de Assis (1839–1908), Euclydes da Cunha (1866–1909), whose Rebellion in the Backlands, first published in 1902, has become perhaps the most widely known work by a Brazilian writer, Graça Aranha (1868–1931), and Coelho Netto (1864–1934), ranks among the best of Portuguese-language literature; and Brazilian writers since, such as Graciliano Ramos, Rachael de Queiroz, Jorge Amado, José Lins do Rego, Lucio Cardoso, Erico Verissimo and João Felicio dos Santos, thanks also to a freedom of expression which exists in Brazil but not in Portugal, are producing more significant and spirited writing than their Portuguese contemporaries. These writers have been influenced, often noticeably so, by advanced European trends in thought, but all of them reflect an essential feeling of nationhood and nationalism.

Although poetry has not evolved in the same way, nor has the modern Brazilian poet attracted anything like the attention which the new Brazilian writer also is commanding not only in the Portuguese but in the Spanish-speaking world as well, at least four modern Brazilian poets, Murilo Mendes, Carlos Drummond de Andrade, Jorge Lima and Manuel Bandeira, have had very great influence and recognition, too, outside Brazil.

In music, drama and sculpture Brazil has produced very few exponents whose names are known much beyond her own borders. Heitor Villa-Lobos, born in 1884, is perhaps the only Brazilian who has made an impression in the international world of music as a composer and conductor. He is best known for his use of folk themes and Afro-Brazilian rhythms, and for his often original orchestrations. Some of his symphonies and symphonic poems have taken a place amongst the repertoire of the world's great orchestras. This is particularly true in the United States; perhaps his best-known work is *Bachianas*. Music also experienced what Brazilian authorities were later to describe as the interference with natural evolution which the painters and other artists suffered.

During the whole of the nineteenth century, only one composer who was then considered to have any distinction emerged. He was Carlos Gomes who attracted the attention of the Second Emperor in 1861. In his twenties he was sent to Italy to study, where he became completely Europeanized; thereafter he never produced anything of any consequence, apart from one opera, *Il Guarany*. This is very much a European interpretation of a Brazilian theme which is still performed in Brazil more as a ritual now than as a serious artistic work. Other Brazilian composers, such as Francisco Mignone, Camargo Guarnieri and Lourenzo Fernandez have, like Villa-Lobos, relied on African rhythms and folk songs for inspiration; but serious Brazilian music is still in its infancy.

The same could be said of drama, although here it is more a process of rebirth. The Brazilians have always loved the popular theatre and the Brazilian *élite* once had a deep interest in serious drama too; and this interest is increasing and widening now. Since the end of the Second World War a number of experimental theatre groups, often highly sophisticated, have sprung up which are attract-ing growing audiences. While they tend to look towards the French playwrights for their material there is also a strong interest in the English theatre. These groups, too, are digging into the archives searching for Brazilian authors, some of whom had been almost forgotten. The great days of the Brazilian theatre were in the late nineteenth century, for drama was another of the Second Emperor's interests. Eleonora Duse came to Brazil in 1885 and Sarah Bernhardt appeared on three occasions.

Although Dom João VI built the first legitimate theatre in the country, in its early days drama was primitive in expression. The actors were, as present-day official Brazilian chronicles primly record: 'Negroes and mulattos; whites only played the parts of foreigners. The "coloureds" disguised themselves with heavy make-up but their hands betrayed them. They were, furthermore, humble people, labourers, and the women prostitutes.' It was a very long time before acting as a profession gained any sort of respect; even today it is not exactly revered. Towards the end of the century the theatre began to acquire a new status with productions of Scribe, Angier and Sardou. But the Brazilian theatre had much earlier beginnings.

The Jesuit missionaries used simple religious plays as a means of teaching the scriptures to the Indians and for almost three hundred years such plays were performed by the priests and monks. It was the only form of theatre in Brazil until the first, often crude, theatrical companies began to appear towards the end of the eighteenth century and slowly evolved to produce the first Brazilian playwrights, such as Gonçalves de Magalhães (1811–82) and Martins Pena (1815–48). But it was not until after 1883 that it acquired any real artistry and it was to decline again in the first decade of the Republic. Its revival only began in the late 1930s.

If, as many Brazilians would claim, the urge for natural expression seething in the early artists was stifled, or misdirected, the work of Antonio Francisco, *Aleijadinho*, was a poignant exception.[11] Brazil has not produced many sculptors and few of these have attracted any attention abroad. Aleijadinho, too, despite the merit of his work, is hardly known outside Brazil. Yet the question one inevitably asks in wonder, after seeing the profusion of his work and the power of his creativeness, is what anguish was it within him that drove him even after he was a man virtually half dead? Not very much is known about him, and a good deal of this has a tinge of legend.

Antonio Francisco da Costa Lisboa was the illegitimate son of a Portuguese carpenter who came to Brazil in 1720 to work in the gold town of Vila Rica, afterwards known as Ouro Prêto. His mother was a Negro slave. He was born in 1738 and records show that when he was twenty-nine years old he was already established as a sculptor working on churches which his father had helped to build, although he seems to have had little conventional teaching. In his late thirties it is believed that he contracted leprosy which, so the stories go, mutilated his feet. Certainly for the rest of his life he was unable to walk and crawled on his hands and knees. Later, his hands, too, were affected and his tools were strapped to his arms. He had to be carried to the site of his work, always wearing a black cloak, his head and face covered. During the last twenty years of his life he was also to become blind, and yet he was still working feverishly two years before his death in 1814 at the age of seventy-six.

His sculptures and carvings in soap stone and in wood of the saints, and on the pulpits and over the porticoes of the baroque churches of Minas Gerais, have a remarkable harmony and delicacy of detail. Perhaps the most haunting expression of his genius is seen in his stone figures of the prophets in the courtyard of the Church of Bom Jesus at Congonhas do Campo, and in the sixty-six life-size wooden figures depicting the Stations of the Cross in Ouro Prêto. But the tradition of Aleijadinho died with him, for sculpture, too, was to be influenced by the French mission which Dom João brought to Brazil. Of its disciples and others who were to come later in the nineteenth century, only Rodolfo Bernadelli achieved any real distinction.

The modernist movement only began after 1920 but, as Brazilians admit, it has not yet produced any very significant exponents.

It is perhaps in architecture[12] that Brazil has made the greatest advance, and it is certainly the adventurousness of men such as Lucio Costa, Oscar Niemeyer, Enrique Mindlin and a score of others who have attracted world attention, particularly since the building of Brasilia began in 1956. Architecture is one aspect of Brazil, a country still unknown in so many other respects, which has been so explored and analysed from every angle and by so many authorities that there is little left to say about it. For almost four hundred years architecture, too, almost exclusively concerned with the building of churches, had been 'passively colonial or sub-European'. Although the Brazilians were influenced by such masters as Le Corbusier, this time they were not dominated; and it is perhaps in their architecture that they have voiced their individuality and revolt more than in any other form of art. It is also an expression of the flamboyance and the desire to impress which are very much ingredients of the Brazilian nature; and it is one face of culture they can show to the world with pride and without earnest explanations as to its origins, or why it did not evolve sooner. It is something new in the way of tropical architecture, and *they* created it.

In the almost five hundred years since Brazil first began to be drawn, almost accidentally, so it might seem, on the map, in these centuries in which her people have evolved, culture, in the accepted sense, appears to have been one of the last features to become discernible in the Brazilian. And yet, a culture much older than that of the Portuguese was being planted in those first years after discovery. Although it was alien soil, too, for those who brought its seeds, it has grown deep roots because of the infinitely greater number of the sowers. They were the African slaves. The Negro brought his gods with him and a primitive art which was expressed in the fashioning of charms and effigies and in the elaborate rituals of worship of pagan saints and demons. It was not exactly culture but it was something tangible, and more dramatically appealing than the God the Church offered. The Church, in fact, realizing that these cults could not be simply eradicated by burning idols or even by persecution, accorded them a respectability by christianizing the black man's faiths. This compromise gave birth to Voodoo which, in its many forms, some of them frightening in their savagery, is practised in Brazil as *macumba*. No ill-fitting mask was ever really pressed hard on to the face of this 'culture'. Although Brazil is a predominantly Roman Catholic country in which less than six per cent of the people profess to have any other faith, or no faith at all, Christianity and macumba coexist. Many a Brazilian today, and not only the coloured, will go dutifully to Mass on Sunday, but during the week he will also have been, just as dutifully, to the *terreiro*, one of the several names for macumba places of worship.

The slave brought not only his physical strength and his gods, but the exuberance of his dancing and music and an enjoyment of life which the native Indian and the Portuguese settler did not have. The Negroes also began very soon to feel at home in a way that the Negroes in North America never did. The feeling of belonging to the land and, on the whole, the kindly treatment they received as slaves, transformed them into perhaps the least inhibited racial elements of a country anywhere; and in great parts of Brazil, of course, they are not a minority either. In their religious beliefs and attitude to life, far from being influenced by the white man they have exercised an influence of their own. It is their music and songs, for instance, and the rhythms of their dancing which have become the folk music of Brazil.

But it is macumba which has seeped deeply into the Brazilian, and it has given God some strange faces too. The way it has spread is a phenomenon which is seriously concerning the Church now, for it is no longer the cult only of the coloured and of the poor. It is said that there are some eight million active adherents but that may be a conservative figure. Even some intellectual Brazilians have turned to it, and they do not practise macumba as an undergraduate might explore, for a time, the excitement of spiritualism. It is an escape from reality, a drug, and something more exhilarating and satisfying than anything the Church has to offer. Its real danger, however, is its effect on that growing number of Brazilians who seem content, at least so far, to live in an inert world apart. In them it is perpetuating an ignorance of a different kind and a sense of fatalism. So many of them are sure that their salvation will come from heaven, but it is not the same heaven which the white man or the rich man talk about. To witness a macumba session can evoke a disturbing reaction: a cross between a guffaw and a vomit. But what is almost more haunting is to see the saucers of food among the flowers and the candles on church altars and to hear, in the quietness of the night, even in the sophisticated surroundings of the city, coming from somewhere in the hills or perhaps even from around the corner of your own street, the sound of the low throb of drums; the reminders of yet another world of Brazil.

10   The Splendid Years

THE YEAR 1961 marked the end of yet another era in Brazil's now headlong progress. Although it had covered a period of just thirty-one years, much more had happened to change Brazilians' lives than in the preceding one hundred and thirty nine years since their independence. The changes in the country, and, above all, in the people, had been even greater than in the three decades which had begun with the emergence of a Republican Brazil on that November night in 1889 when the Empire had quietly died.

In 1930 Vargas had seized power and was to launch his social revolt which awakened in a great many Brazilians an entirely new and rebellious awareness of the social injustice which they had accepted so patiently for so long. An even newer Brazil had begun to emerge before he was deposed fifteen years later by the army after his régime had deteriorated into dictatorship and nepotism. But those fifteen years had changed the mentality of a people, or at least a great part of them, and they certainly changed the whole political structure of a country. Vargas was to return again in 1951, this time as a freely elected president and with an overwhelming majority. The electorate by then had grown to over 11,600,000, but Vargas did not owe his success only to the votes of the ordinary Brazilians who were still confident that he would carry on the interrupted social revolution he had started twenty years earlier. This revolution was the first that they had ever known which had any claims to call itself a social one; and there has never really been another since. But during those fifteen years Vargas had also built a new machine and a new political club in which genuine reformers rubbed shoulders with the merely ambitious and the opportunists. In the election campaign in 1950 many a politician with influence, sceptical about his own party's chances against Vargas's popular appeal, switched his loyalty; even men who had helped to depose him five years before now stood at his side.

Although the Vargas government crashed in dishonour less than four years later, the political organism with insidious tentacles which he had created did not. In 1954 Getulio Vargas, in a gesture which was utterly out of character, committed suicide; but many Brazilians, grief-stricken and stunned though they were, consoled themselves with the thought that the social consciences he had awakened could never be stifled. Inevitably, however, this new awareness, coupled with the immaturity of so many of the electorate even today, also made possible for the first time the emergence of the demagogues which have become the greenfly of Brazilian political reform.

In 1956 came the Kubitscheck government and with it the apparent realization of so many Brazilian dreams. Juscelino Kubitscheck came to power thanks to the support of a large section of the Vargas 'club'. Although he represented the right wing of the *Getulistas*, the communists backed him too, but only because his opponents were either far more right wing, or not worth bothering about. During his five-year term of office Brazilians began to feel that they were watching miracles. Foreign investment poured in and industrialization, which had been growing at a steady pace, broke into a gallop. In addition Brasilia was being built and it was attracting the attention of the world as an example of imaginative experiment and progress. Brazilians had never felt quite so elated. The north was still struggling – in the parched lands of the northeast there had been the discordant note of revolt of the hungry millions in 1958 – and nothing much had happened to change life in the interior either; but the third world of Brazil was booming.

There were other discordant voices in this atmosphere of elation, the warnings of those Brazilians who were totting up the cost of Kubitscheck's building spree and watching the foreign credits and the loans mounting at a pace increasingly out of step with Brazil's earnings. But most Brazilians who were able to bask in the smiling countenance of prosperity could hardly be expected to listen to these pessimists. They were proudly watching the great new industries growing behind the protection of tariff walls; the new hydro-electric power stations, the rising skyscrapers of São Paulo and Rio, and of course Brasilia, which was to open up a vast new area in that rich, empty interior. These were the splendid years. Vargas, with his revolutionary labour code, had given so many Brazilians for the first time a say in their destiny and now Kubitscheck had consummated the transformation of Brazil's economy from its agricultural, almost colonial status, to that of a modern industrial country. It was almost as if Brazil had achieved a second independence, this time an economic one.

During those thirty full years the Second World War had also been fought and Brazil had taken an active part. She entered the war in August 1942 and sent an expeditionary force of over 20,000 men who fought with distinction in the Italian campaign. Hers were the only Latin American troops – in fact, the only non-Europeans, except for the United States and British Dominion troops – ever to fight on European soil. Brazilian airfields and bases were placed at the disposal of the Allies and her air force helped to keep the shipping lanes of the South Atlantic open, because Brazil had also become a valuable source of raw materials and food. For Brazil, the enemy was not so far away either; Dakar was less than 2,000 miles off her northern coast. The war ended, a Brazilian, a former foreign minister, Oswaldo Aranha, was elected President of the General Assembly of the United Nations at San Francisco.

For a country which politically and economically had been forgotten at the crossroads so often, it is understandable that so many Brazilians should have felt a sense of exultation and pride. The present was dazzling enough but the future appeared even brighter, for the splendid years seemed likely to continue even after the Kubitscheck government's five-year term of office ended. Brazilians felt an almost greater sense of achievement when, in October 1960, they elected as his successor Janio Quadros by an overwhelming majority and defeated the government machine for the first time. It might seem paradoxical, almost an act of ingratitude, that Brazilians should have turned against the successor chosen by a government which had brought about the fulfilment of so many dreams. But in the latter part of the Kubitscheck government they were awakening to some disturbing facts. Those warning voices which had once spoken only to the winds about the perils of overspending were being heard at last; and the prophets of gloom were being vindicated now by the evidence of inflation and its effects on the everyday lives particularly of middle-class Brazilians. There were also ugly stories of mismanagement and corruption and many of them were to be proved true.

In 1961, when Janio Quadros took office, Brazilians again glowed with hope that now they had a president who was not contaminated by or committed to any political or financial clique. That was certainly true. Janio, as he was known throughout Brazil – Brazilians usually refer to public figures by their Christian names – did not owe allegiance even to a political party. He was a real independent, the sort of man whom Brazilians had long been looking for, and he was truly elected by the will of the people. The government candidate was a soldier and the former war minister, Marshal Teixeira Lott, and many Brazilians felt that Janio's triumph, and theirs, had been a double one.

No Brazilian president, not even Vargas, had come to office on such a wave of enthusiasm as Janio did. And the enthusiasm was not confined to any particular section, nor was it the hysteria of people kneeling in the streets which greeted Vargas in 1951. The welcome the Brazilians gave Janio was a warm and considered one. He had campaigned on the pledge to eradicate corruption which in its many forms was a blight so widespread that Brazilians had come to accept it as something far more unconquerable than poverty or illiteracy. The symbol of Janio's campaign had been a broom to ram home his promise to sweep Brazil clean. As governor of the state of São Paulo he had earned the reputation of being not only an able, but also a scrupulously honest administrator. The Brazilians were sure that what he had done for São Paulo he could now do for Brazil.

The story of his downfall, of his mistakes and frustrations, must be told later and in the context of these thirty years, but when he resigned barely seven months after taking office, Brazil suffered not so much a political as a moral crisis. In those seven months, Janio had already done a good deal to justify the high hopes which so many Brazilians had had in him. He had begun to introduce austerity measures and above all a new morality in the country's administration and at all levels. His measures were obviously far from popular with the people affected, but most Brazilians began to feel a glow of pride of a different sort. Brazil, it seemed to them, was not only still safely on the road to prosperity; under Janio's guiding hand it would be a saner progress than it had been in the previous five years. Corruption, too, was being tackled now and for the first time as a problem comparable to inflation or disease. When, on 25 August 1961, he resigned, Brazilians experienced a great many emotions, but psychologically the most corroding one was the recurrence of the sense of insecurity, the sickening feeling of being betrayed once again.

With Janio's resignation, the splendid years seemed suddenly to have become meaningless. In almost any other country in Latin America the atmosphere and the problems he left behind him might well have erupted into civil war. He was succeeded by the vice-president, João Goulart, a man who was suspected not only by the right wing but by every moderate thinking Brazilian and by a big majority of the armed forces too. Goulart – or Jango, as Brazilians had always known him – was not only the personification of Getulismo, for he had been one of Vargas's most devoted disciples, he was a textbook example of the demagogue. But, characteristically, the country did not fall apart in revolt. Goulart's constitutional right to assume full powers was eventually upheld, after the failure of a compromise measure to curb his personal power which was the introduction of a short-lived parliamentary form of government. It was almost three years later, when Brazil's finances were in a state of chaos and Goulart had reached far out to the left and to the communists for support, before he and his government were deposed. As usual, a group of army officers, joined by civilian politicians, hatched the plot and it was the military who quietly carried out the execution on 1 April 1964 – and preserved the peace. Most Brazilians never really knew what was taking place until it was all over.

These years in which so much had happened to the Brazilians also witnessed a complete turn of the political wheel. They began with what had been for many of them a social revolt. They ended with a right-wing Revolutionary government with a soldier, General Castelo Branco, as its head and the military once again exercising, but now openly so, their role of police dog. Outright or even suspected left-wing and communist elements were removed not only from the political stage but also from any position in which they might catch the public eye. The competition to carry out the building of the new Brazil had now been taken over by different factions of the right.

In 1964 a great many Brazilians had been shocked by the mis-management and the often blatant demagogy of the Goulart govern-ment. Financially, Brazil had never been in such straits; in fact, few countries in the world have ever got themselves so deeply in debt as she had done. Even the characteristic optimism of the Brazilians that everything is bound to turn out right in the end had begun to wear thin. Those Brazilians whose interest in economics was restricted to the amount of their grocery bills had plenty to be alarmed about, too. During the thirty-one months the Goulart government lasted, the cost of living soared by more than 300 per cent. Speculators ran happily wild, hoarding and reselling food to each other while the housewives queued to buy even basic necessities. Nobody needed much convincing that it was all due to the mismanagement, or worse, of the Goulart government.

On the whole, even working-class Brazilians helped to put out the flags when the army marched in and took over. The new govern-ment was a coalition of military and civilian leaders who had long opposed Goulart and all he stood for, and there is no doubt about the spontaneous enthusiasm with which it was greeted. But later, Brazilians did begin to query the extent of the blame which these new leaders were also to lay on the shoulders of the left wing and their alleged communist allies. Could the country have been so near to a Cuban-style revolution and a communist take-over as the new government claimed? That was a question which many Brazilians found difficult to answer and it began to worry them even more as they watched the succession of arrests and the suspension of political rights, after secret trials at which the accused were not present, of men like Juscelino Kubitscheck. Because of his personal record of achievement, Kubitscheck was regarded as the strongest candidate for president in the 1964 election; an election which was not to take place. There were a score of others who were dealt with in the same way and whose only crime seemed to be their non-membership of the new political club which had now been founded.

Many Brazilians were aware, but often only vaguely so, of the threat of communism or, what was more likely, popular revolt. (Liberal-thinking Brazilians knew why such threats existed.) In fact, there was plenty of evidence, if only they had cared to look more closely, that the country was drifting away to political and economic chaos. And yet, after the military *coup* in April 1964, what many Brazilians very soon began to wonder was whether this danger might not be exploited by the right wing now and used as a justification for stifling democracy to death. Although democracy in Brazil is no longer a seedling, it is still far from being a robust plant and there are Brazilians who feel that so many of their countrymen are still not ready for it. To understand these feelings one must go back to the events of the past thirty-four years. But meanwhile these suspicions, which Brazilians in 1964 were already turning over in their minds, pointed to one of the biggest problems confronting a government of the right, representing, as this new régime did, a class which the mass of Brazilians had learned to mistrust. To them, such a government seemed even more incompatible with the mood of the country and the times than the Empire had become with a wholly republican continent at the close of the nineteenth century.

62 This stone sculpture of the Prophet Jonah in the courtyard of the Church of Bom
Jesus at Congonhas do Campo by the mulatto *Aleijadinho* dates from the eighteenth
century.

63 This drawing of a sugar mill is by Franz Post, one of the Dutch artists brought to Brazil in the seventeenth century.

64 These mosaics on the offices of *O Estado* newspaper in São Paulo are by the contemporary artist Di Cavalcanti.

65 The Brazilian artist Cândido Portinari has achieved an international reputation.

66 The museum of modern art at Rio de Janeiro is encouraging interest in new painting and sculpture.

67 Oscar Niemeyer, Brazil's foremost architect, was responsible for much of Brasilia's architecture. 68 President Kubitscheck (1956–61) consummated the idea of building a new capital at Brasilia.

69 Blocks of flats in Brasilia.

70 The Cathedral in Brasilia, with its concrete ribs and glass walls, designed by
Oscar Niemeyer.

71 This sculpture outside the presidential palace in Brasilia is by Cesschiatti.

72 Much of Brazil's oil potential has yet to be explored. The Mataripe refinery at São Salvador.

73 The steel mill at Volta Redonda in Minas Gerais is the largest in Latin America and produces almost a million tons of steel a year.

74 Brazil's rivers are her major source of power. The Salto Grande power station in São Paulo.

75 The most ambitious scheme to utilize water power is at the Paulo Afonso falls in Minas Gerais.

76 The port of Santos, one of the largest in Latin America, is the ocean gateway to
São Paulo.

11 The Vargas Era

FEW LATIN AMERICAN COUNTRIES, even those who pride themselves on having a democratic régime, could claim to have such a thing in the strict sense of the term. In many of these countries it is a relatively new institution, undergoing a process of adaptation, and one which the traditional ruling classes still find hard to accept. And yet, contradictory as it may seem, the fact is that however much the under-privileged classes may dream of achieving the right of self-determination, it has often happened that they have fared much better under revolutionary régimes which have been far from democratic. The explanation is sadly simple.

The inequalities in the social structure of so many of these countries are such that promises of reform and solicitude for the masses have assured many a dictator an almost instant popular support with which, psychologically too, he could intimidate his conservative opponents. All the conservatives usually did then was to wait until these messiahs had committed sufficient mistakes; and the unsophisticated masses they had promised to deliver, dazzled by the sudden bounty they were receiving in the way of recognition too, had become so irrationally demanding as to make the downfall of these régimes inevitable. Furthermore, the pledges of some of these popular leaders, their passionate declarations of war on corruption, for example, were eventually recognized, even if not by all their followers, as the sort of virtuous resolutions which could be stoned to death with cream puffs. Yet perhaps the greatest indictment of the traditional ruling classes in many of these countries is the fact that however discredited the governments of these dictators were to become, and however many broken promises they left behind them, they are still remembered for one thing: their proclaimed concern for the under‑privileged.

The era of the iron‑fisted dictator and the old‑style military *junta* has ended, but the advent and the spread of democracy since the end of the Second World War did not change the basic attitude of the old ruling oligarchies very much. Democracy did not always imply a new respect for the will of the majority. Very often it simply provided a legal endorsement of the objectives of a minority. So many factors which already existed, or were created for the occasion, could ensure that a voter put his mark in the right square on his ballot paper at election times. Once this was done by intimidation, for it was a long time before voters could believe, and with reason, in the inviolability or even the secrecy of the ballot box. As electorates increased, it could still be done, but differently, by persuasion, which took into account the gullibility of so much of the electorate. This gullibility is by no means as great as it was twenty or even ten years ago. But in the atmosphere of social injustice, the appeal of a really articulate demagogue and opportunist is still strong, particularly in local or congressional elections, and there is one factor which can make an election result far from representative of popular feeling. That is the often very large proportion of the population who are most in need of reforms but who must remain silent because their illiteracy deprives them of the right to be heard when their govern‑ments are being chosen.

This was the state of affairs, and to a far greater degree, which existed in Brazil up to 1930 when Getulio Vargas, as a liberal reformist, stood for president against the official and conservative candidate, Julio Prestes, the representative of the economic interests of São Paulo. They and the great landowners of Minas Gerais too now dominated the economy and the politics of the country. Vargas's platform, like so many of his proclaimed objectives, sounded like pure logic and was infinitely appealing in its simplicity to the great majority of other, far less prosperous, Brazilians, to say nothing of the under‑privileged masses. Vargas had a basic, three‑point policy: to raise standards of living and give labour a new dignity; to eradicate corruption; and thirdly to break the Paulista monopoly of prosperity.

From the point of view of the rest of Brazil, which had been watching São Paulo grow rich into almost a country within a country,
one of his most eye-catching slogans was that the interests of Brazil
could no longer be subordinated to the dictates of the coffee and all
the other millionaires of one state: São Paulo.

This feeling was shared by the army and it ensured the success of
the Vargas revolt. Although it had become increasingly sensitive
about its loss of prestige and resented the often far superior conditions
enjoyed by the militia which some states, especially São Paulo, in
their autonomy had built up, the army supported Vargas for deeper
reasons. It was, and still is, a conscripted army, but it was also a
career open to Brazilians from all parts of the country and the officer
class were acutely aware of the backwardness and the poverty of so
much of the rest of Brazil. They also believed that little would be
done about this so long as the country was virtually ruled by the
inward-looking Paulista economic and political oligarchy.

Vargas seized power in October 1930 in a virtually bloodless,
characteristically Brazilian *coup d'état*. The Brazilians, in the streets,
even to some extent in the streets of São Paulo, accorded him the sort
of delirious welcome which they have always given to any man who
promises to do something for them, whether he is a new president,
a state governor, or just the mayor of some dispirited township in the
interior. Furthermore, Vargas claimed that he, and, once again, the
people had been cheated in the election held that year, by the government machine which had cheated another liberal, Rui Barbosa,
twenty years earlier. In 1930 a large number of Brazilians felt they
had a great deal to celebrate.

One of Vargas's first acts in making good his promise to break the
Paulista 'stranglehold' was to replace all the state presidents by
Federal-appointed governors or *Interventores*. Other elected state
officials were also replaced. State militia were placed under Federal
command; even state flags were banned. It was a drastic but necessary step towards creating a more positive national unity, for Brazil
had always been split by regional loyalties and interests. But this
challenge to the cherished principle of autonomy, added to the fact
that the constitution had been suspended, generated a growing feeling

175

of resentment and suspicion of Vargas's real motives. Even some of his own ministers turned against him, but it was in São Paulo that the resentment finally erupted. In July 1932 the Paulistas revolted.

It was the first and only revolution on the scale of civil war in the whole of Brazil's history. All the energy which the Paulistas had devoted to building their state into the most prosperous region of the country now went into their fight against the rest of Brazil. The proclaimed aim of their revolt was to force Vargas to restore the Constitution; but there were deeper motives. For a time some Paulistas felt that they were fighting for their way of life, perhaps even for their separation, if need be, from the rest of the country. An even uglier side of this revolt was the bitter resentment which some Brazilians, particularly from the northeast, showed towards the Paulistas. The remarkable thing is that São Paulo, with all its resources and energy, did not win, or at least fight on much longer. But it seemed as if suddenly the Brazilians realized the disastrous thing they were doing.

Towards the end of September 1932, less than three months after the fighting had begun, the Paulistas were advancing on Rio, but they were halted. A truce was agreed and later São Paulo surrendered. There were no reprisals and all the rebel leaders were given complete amnesty. Vargas was to be challenged again twice, but for different reasons. The early days of his régime saw the emergence of the Brazilian Communist Party and a fascist movement, the *Integralistas*. The communists were led by Luiz Carlos Prestes who, as a young army captain, had become a legendary figure in the 1920s. He was known as the 'Cavalier of Hope', and in his fight to improve population conditions of the interior he had taken the law into his own hands in a Robin Hood fashion; leading an army which roamed the backlands undefeated for three years. The communists did not regard Vargas as any sort of saviour, but they did see a chance of staking their own claims in the atmosphere of social revolt which he had awakened. In 1934 a series of well-organized communist risings broke out in different parts of the country which were joined, in some cases, by entire regiments in these areas and even by air force cadets in Rio de Janeiro. The two men responsible for putting down the communist rising, General Eurico Gaspar Dutra and a then Colonel of the Air Force, Eduardo Gomes, were to play an impor, tant role in the political scene years later. Dutra was to become president after the Vargas régime fell in 1945 and Eduardo Gomes became the rallying figure of the moderate right wing in the 1950 election in which Vargas returned as president.

Although the communists had to go underground in 1934, and Carlos Prestes went into exile, as a party they re,emerged in the 1945 election and their candidate polled nearly 600,000 votes out of a total of almost six million. They also elected fourteen deputies, one senator and scores of municipal councillors. In 1947, urged by the United States, Brazil broke off relations with Russia and later the Commu, nist Party was banned. But despite legal restrictions the communists were by no means silenced. It is difficult to assess the extent of their influence today; they are very much a power behind the scenes in workers' syndicates, in intellectual circles, in the press, and even in the political world, as their infiltration of the Goulart government was to prove. Their influence is also very evident among the distressed population of the interior, and it is reflected in the activity of leaders of the unofficial Peasant Leagues which, over the past ten years, have emerged in rural areas challenging the rights of the great absentee landowners in a revolt against the almost feudal system which has always existed. Even Vargas could do nothing about that. One of the most formidable of these leaders was Francisco Julião in the northeast. A spell,binder, he became an almost mystical figure and as such very much in tune with the mentality of those unique people of the Sertões, fiercely attached to a land which barely supports them.

Men like Julião have been silenced in the anti,communist purge launched in 1964. But the Peasant Leagues, or rather the spirit of them, remains. In these distressed areas, priests are now trying to combat the eroding effects of poverty on a people who seem unlikely ever to know anything else. Some of them have gone into politics as a means of making their pleas heard, for the concern of some of these new missionaries is not so much with the world to come but with the world of the present; a world which these Brazilians of the interior must somehow endure.

The fascist movement led by Plinio Salgado had a short but intriguing existence. Ordinary Brazilians could not really understand them and they did not like the little they could. Their strutting parades also tickled something which is very strong in the Brazilian nature, a sense of the ridiculous. Because of the colour of the shirts worn by Plinio Salgado's earnest but often confused young followers, they were nicknamed the 'green chickens', which in Portuguese has a derogatory meaning all of its own. Nevertheless, Salgado did build up a far greater following than many Brazilians had realized. But their end came in May 1938 when, having been, so they felt, betrayed by Vargas, Plinio Salgado, with a small band of his greenshirts, tried a short cut to a *coup d'état* of his own by attacking the Presidential Palace and attempting to assassinate Vargas while he slept. By now the army and a great many other people were beginning to have doubts about Vargas. On the night the fascists attacked, he and members of his household, including his young daughter Alzira, in their pyjamas, had to defend themselves for several hours before troops finally came to their rescue.

The fascist plot was the culmination of a period of more widespread unrest which began after the end of the São Paulo revolution. Vargas had agreed to the election of a Constituent Assembly which was to draft a new constitution and elect a president. In 1934 this Assembly adopted a constitution and duly elected Vargas president. But this constitution was such a compromise between those who wanted to retain the autonomy of the states and those who were pressing for greater authority for the Federal government that in the end it pleased nobody and Vargas least of all. Under this constitution a new presidential election was to be held in 1937 and when the campaign began there were three likely candidates: Armando Salles, who represented the old Paulista interests which had been far from squashed; the fascist candidate, Plinio Salgado, and José Américo, the official candidate. From the very start, José Américo, by his vacillation and obvious ineptitude, was virtually laughed off the course. It is perhaps significant that Vargas should have endorsed his choice. The Paulista candidate had little chance, particularly after Vargas had 'discovered' that one of Armando Salles's main sponsors,

General Flores da Cunha, an old political war horse and governor of the state of Rio Grande do Sul, Vargas's own state, was planning a revolt. Vargas sent Federal troops to the south and Flores da Cunha left hurriedly for Uruguay. Only the fascist candidate remained in the running.

The fascists, in one of those dizzy acrobatics of Brazilian politics, had tried hard to persuade Vargas to stand as their candidate. The German and Italian language newspapers, representing the large German and Italian communities in the country, also added their pleas, for by now Nazi Germany and Mussolini's Italy were taking an interest in Brazilian politics. It was only when Vargas refused that Plinio Salgado came forward and, incredible as it might seem, there appeared to be forces in the country strong enough to ensure his election. They certainly impressed Vargas. Already there had been a communist plot so it was not hard for him to organize a successful anti-fascist *coup*. Even though some of the support he got, particularly in the army, was not exactly enthusiastic, the prospect of a fascist government outweighed the suspicions many people now had about his ultimate ambitions.

The election was cancelled. Vargas declared a state of emergency and dissolved the Assembly. The Vargas dictatorship had begun. On the eve of the Second World War, the Germans in particular were still comforted by the belief that he had embraced at least the principles of totalitarianism. They also felt that they had found in Brazil an ally which in time might prove useful in South America. But Vargas was to confound them also. He dissolved all political parties with a special emphasis on the fascists, the Integralistas. It was this that led to Plinio Salgado's act of revenge on the night of 11 May 1938. Attempting to assassinate a man in his bed was despicable enough; but what, characteristically too, turned the Brazilians against the Integralistas even more was the alleged 'evidence' that the plot had been blessed by the German government. Shortly afterwards the Brazilian Foreign Ministry asked for the recall of the German ambassador.

The outbreak of war helped to consolidate Vargas's position. The new constitution which he decreed in 1937, the fourth in Brazil's history, established the *Estado Novo*, a corporate state in which the government acquired wide powers of intervention, particularly in the economic field, to attain social reforms. It also put an end to every expression of autonomy in the states. It was the end, too, of even that degree of democracy which Brazil had attained. The new constitution did not determine Vargas's term of office; all it promised, in effect, was elections when circumstances permitted. Although Vargas never instituted a police state of the sort which has so often stifled life and thought in other parts of Latin America, he came near to doing so. Politics as a subject of conversation above a whisper was banned, but the Brazilians are an irrepressible people. The Brazilian press, too, had always been a courageous one with no inhibitions about expressing its views, and very soon Brazilians were to experience some unfamiliar affronts from censorship to the knock on the door in the middle of the night.

But in those fifteen years Vargas did introduce reforms he had promised. He created the Ministry of Labour, reorganized health and education services and re-started the development of the northeast which had been suspended in 1922. One of his typical projects was the reclamation of the swamplands, the *Baixada Flumeninse*, an area far greater than the Pontine marshes, in the state of Rio, which were drained and turned into farming land. Another was Brazil's first steel mill at Volta Redonda which is still a showpiece and an example of what Brazilians can do in the way of combining industrial progress with social welfare. A carefully landscaped town was built up around the mill with schools, clinics, recreation centres and parks for steel workers, a great many of whom had to be educated and trained from backward peasants. Volta Redonda became a steel mill in a garden and a model for other Brazilian industries.

Vargas laid the foundations of a new progress. This did not, however, spread much beyond regions which had already been developing, even though his proclaimed aim had been to break down regional concepts. But, above all, he gave the working classes, in the towns at least, a sense of security. Considering they had never had such a thing before, he did not have to give them very much. In fact, some of the pension and insurance schemes he started existed more in theory than in practice and their funds often disappeared in loans for private speculative investments.

Unhappily, the labour code he introduced in 1943 also gave the factory and office worker a sense of perhaps too easy security. It empowered the government to decree minimum wages, instituted obligatory severance pay and labour courts which were usually on the side of the employee. Perhaps, however, the biggest inducement of all to abuse was the provision that a man who had worked for the same employer for ten years became virtually an office fixture and almost impossible to dismiss. But in the fields of education, health, in fact, legitimate social security, the working-class Brazilian did not achieve very much. As the cities grew, so did the slums and the *favelas*, the shanty towns. Despite Vargas's proclaimed concern for agriculture, the rural population were also still a forgotten people. And yet the mass of Brazilians were deeply grateful to their champion. He was the first they had ever had and they believed him when he blamed others for his failure to give them more.

It is hard to analyse Vargas's political philosophy, or even to dis-tinguish which of his acts were prompted by conviction and which were dictated merely by expediency. Perhaps the biggest mistake an analyst could make would be to attribute to him any very profound or sociological reasoning. Although Vargas was an astute politician who understood the Brazilians better than they did themselves, his greatest talent was perhaps the directness of his reasoning. He was in many ways a simple man, ill at ease with foreigners, and who mistrusted experts and 'clever men'. He chose as his advisers people whose mentalities were almost replicas of his own; and their loyalty in his eyes compensated for their shortcomings. He could also judge the right moment when firmness could be profitably sacrificed to flexibility. The army had grown to mistrust him, yet he retained its tolerance for fifteen years. Despite all he had said about the Paulista economic oligarchy he also won their tolerance by not interfering too much with their prosperity. He pacified coffee interests by buying up their surplus production and so guaranteeing prices. In the six years after 1931 almost a third of São Paulo's coffeee harvest was bought by the government and burnt. He was also a master of dividing his opponents and he did not hesitate to use as blackmail the prospect of a popular rising and likely civil war if he were deposed or even obstructed.

Getulio Dornelles Vargas was a farmer's son. Born on 19 April 1883, he grew up in those stormy confused days of the first republic. He became a lawyer, went into politics before he was thirty and rose to become president of his home state of Rio Grande do Sul and Minister of Finance in the Washington Luiz government which he was to overthrow. Whether he was a sincere reformer or merely wanted power for power's sake is also hard to say; perhaps he sought a combination of the two. His favourite pastime was to spend long afternoons on the veranda of his ranch chatting endlessly with friends, although he had few close friends, content in the quiet atmosphere of the farm. He often seemed to regard the whole of Brazil as a 'farm' in which everyone was content, or at least did not intrude on his own peace of mind. Although he was a man of undoubted courage, he would often sacrifice principles for the sake of peace and quiet; and this tolerance was to breed a corruption in his two governments which was his undoing in the end. Although, as some of his harshest critics will concede, his own hands remained clean of its shoddier forms.

In 1945 Brazilians were experiencing some exhilarating emotions. The war in defence of freedom and democratic liberties, in which they had fought, too, had just ended. It was time, they felt, to fight the same sort of war at home. Vargas's popularity with the still eagerly hopeful masses was as high as ever, but the silenced press, the army and a growing number of liberal-thinking Brazilians were in no mood for blackmail now. The press led the way. Disregarding the law of censorship, it began to publish blistering attacks on the dictator, a word which had never been used before in connection with Vargas, at least, not publicly. Vargas seemed to be genuinely shocked and distressed by the venom of these attacks and he announced abruptly that he would retire. He also named 2 December as the date for the election of his successor. It was the signal for an explosion of popular demonstrations demanding that he should remain. There was also feverish activity among those politicians who had become so identified with his régime that a future without Vargas seemed dim indeed. The army, grown wary of Vargas's tactics and remembering 1937, was not prepared to take any chances. In the hours of darkness of 29 October, just as they had done on that November night back in 1889 when the Empire was quietly put to death, they surrounded the Presidential Palace. When the army delegation presented itself to demand Vargas's resignation, he was waiting for them, his resignation ready. As usual, most Brazilians only knew what had happened when they woke up the next morning to learn from their newspapers that the dictatorship was over. On that day a great many people danced in the streets again, but in the shanty towns and in other dark corners of Brazil there were many more who wept.

77 Getulio Vargas seized power in 1930 and ruled Brazil both as dictator and president for eighteen years.

78 Demonstrations in Rio in August 1942 against the axis powers a few days before Brazil entered the Second World War.

79 Vargas gained strong popular support throughout the country. He is seen here talking to young Brazilians.

80 He introduced reforms particularly in the social field. Here he is being shown a model of the new Technical School of Aviation in 1942.

81 But his basic concern was to raise standards of living and give labour a new dignity. Vargas talking to industrial workers.

82 Communist and fascist agitation erupted in the 1930s. A group of arrested fascists who attempted to assassinate Vargas in 1938 under guard.

83 Riots in Rio de Janeiro after Vargas's suicide in 1954; crowds burning vans of the anti-Vargas newspaper *O Globo*.

84 The political carnival of election time in Brazil; campaign banners in Rio de Janeiro in 1959.

85 Janio Quadros (*centre*) remained president for seven months in 1960-1. Ex-president Kubitscheck (*right*) and vice-president João Goulart (*left*).

86 João Goulart was president for three years until his overthrow by the army in 1964. The arrest in Rio of one of Goulart's army supporters.

87 There had been strong feelings amongst a section of Brazilian workers in 1959 in support of the Cuban Revolution.

88 Bank clerks demonstrating for better wages and conditions in 1960.

89 A meeting of the National Assembly in Brasilia in 1964.

90 A leader of the Revolt of the Right in 1964 which overthrew Goulart's left-wing régime was Carlos Lacerda, governor of Guanabara. These were some of his civilian supporters.

91 Naval units triumphantly toured Rio de Janeiro after the success of the 1964 Revolution.

92 Soldiers guard the Brazilian Congress as General Castelo Branco is nominated president after the 1964 Revolution.

93 The mission of the Castelo Branco government and all successive governments is to arouse in Brazil's millions a new sense of destiny and purpose and to bring cohesion to this vast and socially divided land.

12   Democracy and the Jerk to Reality

IN THE NINETEEN YEARS between the overthrow of the first
Vargas régime and the Revolt of the Right of 1964, Brazil had six
presidents of which only two completed their terms of office. Admittedly, one of these six, João Café Filho, had not been elected. As the
vice-president, he automatically succeeded Vargas when he committed suicide in 1954, but he was driven from office by the army
within fifteen months. Another was João Goulart who was vice-
president when Janio Quadros resigned in 1961, barely seven months
after his inauguration. Goulart remained in office less than three
years and his overthrow, again by the army, was the most spectacular,
although characteristically bloodless, *coup d'état* which Brazil has
witnessed. These were an eventful nineteen years; and yet they were
not as chaotic, as far as Brazil's material progress was concerned, as
this succession of interrupted governments would imply, and they
will be remembered not so much for the return of Vargas in the
election of 1950 as for his three successors: Kubitscheck, the builder;
Quadros, the moral reformer; and Goulart, the unwitting under-
taker at the funeral of the left. During these years the new pattern of
Brazilian politics also emerged and it began to take shape during the
election campaign of 1945.

The shock of Vargas's overthrow in that same year was soon to be
almost forgotten, at least in political circles, in the excitement over
the return of democracy. Even before elections were announced the
scramble to reform old political groups and to assemble new parties

193

had begun. It was not just a thankful celebration for the return of constitutional rights, it was to become an orgy. Of the confusion of parties which sprang up, most of them incorporating the words 'social' or 'labour' in their names, in deference to the social conscious- ness which Vargas had aroused, three parties emerged and have survived to represent the main political forces rather than clearly defined doctrines in the country. The largest, the PSD Social Democratic Party, represented the conservative element; the UDN National Democratic Union was also conservative, but included some rather more liberal spirits; and the PTB Brazilian Labour Party endorsed, rather than actually founded, by Vargas. Its strength lay not in the number of its members but in its identification with Vargas.

The problem facing the main parties in 1945 was to find candi- dates who would impress the electorate as being like Vargas in social outlook. But the army insisted that there should be no more Vargas's, although they also appreciated that a candidate would not have much hope of success if he were too identified with the conservatives. As the army also insisted that this election should be a scrupulously fair one, the ideal seemed to be a coalition candidate. But the prob- lem of finding a man who could meet so many requirements and still face the ultimate test of the ballot box seemed insoluble. The solution, of course, was a soldier: General Eurico Gaspar Dutra, who had been Vargas's Minister of War. He was unassuming and respected for what he was, a professional soldier. More important still, he had no political ambitions. His only serious rival was Eduardo Gomes, now a brigadier in the air force. (Both men had been prominent in putting down the communist rising in 1934.) Gomes represented the 'Liberal' Democratic Union, which was, however, opposed to Vargas's brand of liberalism. Dutra, as the conservative Social Democratic candidate but also supported by Vargas's Labour Party, won by a majority of more than a million votes over his rival; the only other candidate to make any impression on the voters was Yedo Fiuza, the Communist Party candidate, who incidentally was not a communist. It was the last time that the communists were to participate in an election as a party, for in 1947 they were outlawed. In this same election Vargas was voted a senator and he retired, apparently resignedly, to his farm in the far south.

The Dutra government was unspectacular, although it was the first ever to launch the idea of a co-ordinated development programme, the carefully worked out SALTE[13] Plan, which was to have been a long-term attack on four of Brazil's greatest problems: the lack of transport, malnutrition, disease, and the growing need to increase production of power and fuel. It called for an expenditure the equivalent then of nearly £400 million during the next four years. But it made no provisions for coping with a fifth problem: education. Like so many of Brazil's plans it was soon gasping for funds. Brazil's fifth constitution also came into being in the first year of the Dutra government and it restored all the democratic guarantees and civil rights which Vargas had stifled. It has remained in force ever since, although it was to suffer amendments when Quadros resigned, and even more drastic ones after the *coup d'état* of 1964. Dutra also broke off relations with the Soviet Union and banned the Communist Party. He also introduced some pet moral reforms of his own. Gambling was declared illegal and the great casinos of Rio, at the time among the most splendid in the world, were closed overnight. It was a blow to Rio's tourist trade from which it has never really recovered, for Rio had been the Monte Carlo of South America. A noble attempt was even made to outlaw prostitution.

But, above all, Dutra gave Brazil five years of political peace and without resorting to the kind of punitive methods which Brazil was to witness in the first months of the revolutionary government of 1964. That was perhaps his greatest achievement. The presidential term of office was now extended to five years, but long before the campaign for the next election in October 1950 was officially due to open the politicians were feverishly hunting for his successor. An amendment to the constitution now prevented a president from standing for re-election, not that Dutra had any such intention. Perhaps one of the happiest photographs ever taken of him was on the day he handed over the band of office to his successor. To Brazilians who had expected much more from the return of democracy, the Dutra government had seemed stolid and uninspiring.

Brazil was also experiencing the economic effects of the post-war years, and the government was being blamed for the rising cost of living and an inflationary spiral which, in fact, had begun during the war in Vargas's days. Nevertheless, a very large number of Brazilians wanted Vargas back.

To a great many politicians and to the army, to say nothing of those Brazilians who had experienced Vargas's persecution and who had worked hard not only to re-establish democracy but to eradicate the corrosive effects of Vargas's demagogy, it was a shocking prospect. Prodded by the army, the main parties attempted to find a coalition candidate, but this time without success. Even the Church added its warning voice, accusing the Brazilian Labour Party, and indirectly Vargas, of being communist-influenced and a moral danger. As political negotiations distintegrated in a confusion of divided loyalties and secret pacts, popular support for Vargas grew. In the end, Vargas stood as the candidate of his own PTB (Brazilian Labour Party) and of the PSP (Social Progressive Party), founded by another notable demagogue, Adhemar de Barros, who had become governor of São Paulo in 1947. (By 1961, however, Barros, with characteristic foresight, had begun to turn to the right. He was to play a decisive role, when he was again governor of São Paulo, in the overthrow of the Goulart government three years later.) Once again, Eduardo Gomes stood for the 'liberal' UDN and two other smaller parties. The conservative PSD candidate was Christiano Machado who had the support of six parties. A lone orthodox socialist, João Mangabeira, stood for the PSB (Brazilian Socialist Party).

If any evidence was needed that Brazilians, when choosing a president, vote not for parties but for personalities and images, the 1950 election provided it. Although in many ways Vargas's two main opponents, particularly Eduardo Gomes, had more precise and rational policies to offer, Vargas gained 3,829,000 votes. Gomes polled 2,288,000 and Machado, the Conservative, trailed behind them with 1,653,000. The orthodox socialist, João Mangabeira, polled 9,465 votes. Another factor which contributed to Vargas's victory was that many minor but astute political leaders, although officially committed to their own candidates, could sense the result of the race long before it started. Among their supporters they made no secret about where their 'true' sympathies lay, and such leaders could and to some extent still can control often large *blocs* of votes. In Congress, however, the P S D and the U D N won between them 228 seats while the two 'popular' parties, the P T B and P S P secured only 96.

Vargas returned to power in circumstances which would seem to make his government virtually powerless. In Congress he had a solid opposition and the army, too, looked on tight-lipped and menacing. The mass of Brazilians, however, and particularly those barred from the polling booths because of their illiteracy and who could only show their approval after the election by kneeling in the streets, gave him a delirious welcome. The extent of Vargas's magic and the respect for his ability to confound his enemies can be judged by the devout hopes, quite openly expressed even by some of his opponents, that Congress would not be too hostile lest he be tempted to take matters again into his own hands. Many people appeared to have few doubts that he could. But it was a different Vargas who returned in 1950. Although he had campaigned vigorously enough, the fire in him seemed somehow to have been dampened. He, too, intro-duced a plan for social and economic reform which was acclaimed as boldly realistic and called for an expenditure of almost £360 million over the next five years.

It was obviously impossible to carry out such a plan without a great deal of foreign aid and investment. The structure of Brazil's economy had begun to change with the advent of industrialization. This structure was, however, still very unbalanced. Coffee produced the bulk of Brazil's foreign exchange and the backwardness of her agriculture obliged her to import food. Her nationalistic policies, which barred foreign capital from exploring her natural resources, meant that she also had to spend huge sums, for example, on the purchase of foreign oil. Brazil's population was also increasing at a faster pace than production and it all helped to create an economic picture which was not exactly inspiring to potential foreign investors. Soon there was to be a growing feeling of unrest among working-class

Brazilians as the cost of living climbed and life generally became more difficult. This was not what they had expected from Vargas. To pacify them, there were government-decreed wage increases, but thanks to speculation, which ran wild, and other inevitable factors bred by the unbalanced economy, wages and prices played leapfrog and disillusionment mounted.

Since the Second World War the pattern of Brazil's foreign relations had changed, too. The role which Britain and other European countries had played in her economy and trade had been taken over by the United States. But Washington was suspicious of Vargas. When he seized power in 1930 it was some time before the United States would recognize his government and the Brazilians in turn soon began to suspect the United States. She had become the only source of aid and investment on any scale and Brazilians felt that both were being used to apply a stranglehold on their economy. Brazil was not the only Latin American country to have these feelings, and what intensified resentment in the Brazilians was not so much the Americans' veiled hostility towards Vargas but the way in which they seemed to assume the right to dictate policies to the Latin Americans; these poor relations in what Washington liked to call the American family of nations. The often clumsy and, as Latin Americans saw it, patronizing behaviour of some American officials and businessmen made them fume; and it built up an attitude of smouldering resentment. In Cuba it exploded. The United States have not been able to break down this wall of suspicion which has grown between her and almost all the other members of the 'American family', despite the new approach to Latin American problems and susceptibilities which President Kennedy tried to introduce with his long-term and generous programme of aid, the Alliance for Progress, Latin America's equivalent of the Marshall Plan. But even this did not wholly convince the Latin Americans, and in particular the Brazilians, that the plan was simply an attempt to help them to help each other to put their economic house in order. Nevertheless, when President Kennedy died, Latin Americans felt they had suffered a personal loss, for slowly an understanding of the change in American policy was beginning to dawn on them. Then in 1965 came the American intervention in Santo Domingo and all the old suspicions flared up again.

During the Vargas government American credits and investment did continue but they were not on a scale to make very much differ- ence to an economy which needed a basic overhauling; and Vargas and his advisers were not able to do this. But that was only one contributory factor to his downfall. In and out of Congress and in the armed forces there were people who, looking back into a not so distant past, could not accept Vargas in power even as a constitu- tionally elected president. But there were many others, and their numbers grew as the months went by, who were genuinely revolted by the corruption which his régime was breeding. Whether Vargas really knew what was happening in the back rooms of his govern- ment, or to what extent he was directly involved in subsequent events, are questions which have never been satisfactorily answered; but the mounting feeling of disgust erupted in a way which nobody had quite expected, and it stirred something in the hitherto tolerant Brazilians which was to flare up again seven years later and put an end to the Goulart government. It was this awakened feeling of revolt against corruption which swept Janio Quadros, the moral reformer, into power in 1961.

One of the most fierce opponents Vargas ever had was Carlos Lacerda, a member of the UDN, who was to become governor of the new state of Guanabara, and later a prominent leader in the Revolt of the Right in 1964. During the Vargas government, however, it was as a journalist that he made his mark and his attacks on the corruption of the government were often so violent that many Brazilians tended to dismiss them as the ravings of a neurotic. But Lacerda had tenacity as well as tremendous courage and, despite threats on his life and occasional arrests, he persisted in his cam- paign. On the night of 5 August 1954 members of Vargas's personal guard planned to silence him by assassination. In the ambush they laid for him Lacerda was wounded but his companion, a young air force officer, was killed. An inquiry carried out by the air force virtually at gun-point, for the government seemed reluctant to act, dredged up some shocking revelations of the extent of the corruption

199

which Lacerda had been denouncing for so long; and it involved people very close to the president. The crowds came out into the streets again, but this time to demand Vargas's resignation.

During the next eighteen days, as more shattering disclosures were published, the feeling of shame and resentment grew. Military leaders urged Vargas to resign, but he refused. In the end he agreed to relinquish the presidency for ninety days so that a full inquiry could be carried out. This was at dawn on 25 August, and four hours later he was found dying in his bedroom by his son. He had shot himself in the heart. But Vargas left a letter and when that was made public, barely two hours after his death, and it was read out repeatedly over the government radio throughout that morning, many Brazilians who had been clamouring for his resignation now began to howl for vengeance against 'Vargas's assassins'. In this letter Vargas claimed that his struggle to liberate the people had been continuously opposed by foreign interests allied with certain Brazilian interests bent on preventing the emancipation of the masses. It was a long letter, filled with calculated inflammatory phrases: 'the people are now defenceless'; 'hour by hour I fought for you'; and there were references also to the 'great profits of foreign firms'. It ended with what many Brazilians have come to regard as his epitaph:

. . . I gave you my life, now I give you my death. I chose this way to defend you, for my soul will be with you, my name shall be a flag for your struggle. This people to whom I have been a slave will never be anyone's slaves again. I take the first step to eternity. I leave life to enter history.

With that letter and a bullet in the heart Vargas passed not just into history, he became a part of Brazilian folk-lore. But in that week after his death Brazil came perilously near to civil and class war. There were riots. American property was destroyed, for the mob were quick to identify the Americans as the 'foreign interests' Vargas had denounced, and foreigners, if they were wise, stayed at home. It was thanks to the last-minute unity of the armed forces, for Vargas still had friends in the army, that disaster did not result.

There were still fourteen months to go before the election of a new

president was due, but in the meantime there were state, congres/
sional and municipal elections. These were held on 3 October, less
than two months after Vargas's death, and they provided an interest/
ing, if bewildering, study of political behaviour and Brazilian
reactions. Once again it was an orgy of democracy. All told, there
were more than 60,000 candidates which included professional foot/
ballers, radio comedians and popular song writers; for politics had
become a rewarding calling in more ways than one. In Rio alone
there were 1,200 contenders for 69 seats in the municipal council.
Some candidates, hopefully exploiting the emotion aroused by
Vargas's death, campaigned in deep mourning; others used pictures
of Vargas's coffin on their posters. But the electorate was to confound
them. In Congress the PSD and the UDN gained the majority of
seats. In São Paulo an anti/Vargas candidate was elected governor;
he was Janio Quadros. In Rio, Carlos Lacerda defeated Vargas's
own son in the election for mayor and in other parts of the country,
even in Vargas's home town, Vargista candidates were defeated.

In the presidential election the following year, however, Juscelino
Kubitscheck was elected with João Goulart as vice/president. Al/
though the PSD candidate he was also supported by the Vargista
machine and by the communists. It was not a decisive victory. He
polled only a few hundred thousand more votes than his nearest
rival, the Church/endorsed candidate, Juarez Távora. To the army,
and in particular the air force, it seemed as if Vargas's ghost was
walking as Kubitscheck's shadow. There was a movement to
prevent his inauguration but the armed forces, although again
divided, moved in to ensure that the verdict of the polls should be
respected. In this anti/Kubitscheck plot, the interim president, Café
Filho, a placid, good/natured northeasterner, found himself some/
how involved. He was deposed and placed under house arrest and
was to provide one of those touches of comedy which have so often
been the blessed relief of some of Brazil's most tense moments.
Confined to his flat, he used to appear at the window, at regular
intervals, always in pyjamas, to wave to his friends and supporters,
and so became known as the Cuckoo Clock president. The pyjamas
were a gesture of consideration to his guards, for, as he explained:

'If I appear in a collar and tie the good fellows panic, thinking I am going to run away.'

On 31 January 1956 Juscelino Kubitscheck was duly inaugurated in one of the most splendid and costly ceremonies Brazilians had ever witnessed, and it set the tone of his government. Before his inauguration he had visited Europe and the United States to explain the new Brazil he intended to build and he was the first Brazilian president ever to promote his country in this way. He certainly impressed his listeners, particularly in the United States, and the result was a flood of foreign investment. Much of it went into new industries but there were also credits to finance his new roads and power stations and, of course, Brasilia.

Kubitscheck had been a successful surgeon before he took up politics as a career and became governor of Minas Gerais. His solution for inflation and Brazil's other ills was to go all out to increase the country's productive capacity, even if it meant more inflation and heavy foreign debts in the meantime. As a result of this policy the gross national product rose by almost six per cent a year. Industry advanced at such a pace that Brazil became virtually self-sufficient in consumer goods and very nearly so in industrial equipment. She still, however, had to import oil and food. This new prosperity was also not shared by the great mass of Brazilians. The price of a policy of expansion at any cost, in terms of foreign indebtedness alone, left Brazilian economic planners with a problem new only in its scale, but all the more grave because foreign earnings continued to be very largely dependent on coffee alone. This was a commodity at the mercy of world prices and increasingly threatened by new suppliers.

It was in this atmosphere of boom and warning signs of crises ahead and ugly stories of mismanagement and corruption that Janio Quadros campaigned for the presidency in 1960 and won over 48 per cent of the votes; the highest majority ever achieved by a Brazilian president. Although he had refused to commit himself to any party, political leaders soon realized that his appeal was messianic; and, led by the UDN, a succession of parties, including some of the members of the PTB, lined up behind him, forsaking their own candidate, the government nominee, Marshal Lott. Yet, despite Quadros's tremendous appeal, the average voter seemed to know little about his policies, which, in fact, were not very different from those of his main rival, Marshal Lott. What they did know, however, was that he had always been scrupulously honest. Quadros had been a schoolteacher and was a man of considerable intellect. He was also a showman. In his efforts to indentify himself with the ordinary Brazilian he often campaigned in an old suit and with holes in his shoes which his more unkind critics claimed he had cut himself. But he was a man with a genuine mission; a radical reformer who looked like a tramp and talked like a don.

Quadros had often been at loggerheads with the traditional political establishment as governor of São Paulo, but he had managed to neutralize the hostility of the politicians by appealing directly to the people and he certainly gave São Paulo one of the best governments it ever had. He obviously intended to employ the same tactics as president, for he felt that what Brazil most needed was a government with authority unencumbered by purely political considerations. This created an almost immediate opposition against him in Congress. The independent foreign policy he advocated, which included closer relations with the communist world for the sake of widening Brazil's trade partnerships, and his sympathetic attitude towards Cuba, also worried even some moderate left-wing Brazilians. The Americans were frankly shocked.

His abrupt resignation on 25 August 1961 seemed to have been a calculated move to get the authority he felt he needed and to put Congress in its place. He apparently believed that the mass of Brazilians would clamour for his return and on his own terms. But the clamour never came. His resignation was promptly accepted by Congress and the feeling he left in the minds of Brazilians was that while they did appreciate that he had been harassed by Congress and by the entrenched right wing, he should have been man enough to stand up to it and so justify, but not abuse, the trust so many of them had placed in him; for they also believed now that he had tried to force on them an authoritarian government of his own. In a sullen, resentful silence which had fallen on the country, Janio Quadros sailed for England and into voluntary exile. He returned again the following year, but the Brazilians had not forgiven him. Yet four years later it was evident, particularly in the state of São Paulo, that many Brazilians would like to see him back in politics. They may not have forgiven him entirely but they had not forgotten the good he had done or had tried to do.

João Goulart, the vice-president, 'Jango' the demagogue, the personification of *Getulismo*, was now Brazil's new president and there were over four years to go before the next election was due. A great many Brazilians were appalled and in the mood for rebellion. But once again the Constitution was upheld and Goulart was duly sworn in, and eventually given full powers. Few Brazilian presidents have had to face quite the same kind of opposition or the mistrust with which his every move was watched, even by some of his own supporters. The alliances and counter-alliances he attempted to make would have been too intricate even for Vargas to cope with, and they only added to the conviction that he was an opportunist far too involved with the extreme left and that his ultimate aim was to resurrect the Vargas régime, or create a clumsy and even more dangerous replica of it.

His final undoing, however, was the agrarian reform he tried to force. This was drastic and might have been effective but it also meant placing enormous power in the hands of the Federal government. It would have been the sole administrator of the plan, and with the right to expropriate any land it thought fit. Compensation was to be made in government bonds redeemable in twenty years, but inflation could have made payment of this kind amount to virtual confiscation. Even Brazilians who were in favour of drastic reform felt it was far too dangerous left in the hands of a man like Goulart. But he was also demanding congressional approval for the enfranchisement of those illiterate millions, and for a Bill enabling him to stand for re-election. If Goulart counted on a wave of popular support for his policies he was to be bitterly disillusioned, as Quadros had been. When his government fell on 1 April 1964, and he eventually fled to Uruguay, he was a lonely man indeed. He had been abandoned even by some of his closest friends. But, true to form, what had also turned many Brazilians against him was his alleged plan to invoke the help of 'foreign' communists and Cuban agitators in carrying out his ambitions.

Brazilians had not recovered from the 'Quadros betrayal', and for a long time they seemed to regard the politics of the Goulart government almost with indifference, although they were becoming increasingly bitter about the more direct effects of his mismanagement, the speculation, and the soaring prices. The Revolt of the Right in April 1964 was the jerk to reality in more ways than one. To so many Brazilians the splendid years of the Kubitscheck government and all the fun of the circus of democracy and their protest against corruption, and the power of the government machine which they had demonstrated so confidently in their election of Janio Quadros, seemed like a dream now as the new government firmly began to take matters into its own hands. Once again, ordinary Brazilians were relegated to the role of spectators. It is true that Congress was still there, but as the Revolutionary government started its political spring-clean and made other changes about the house, many Brazilians began to wonder just how long Congress would survive.

The policies of the new government were simple and familiar. There were to be sweeping reforms, including financial and agrarian reforms but, above all, a fumigation of subversion and corruption – communism and getulismo came under both headings – and it was to be done by a hastily drafted amendment to the Constitution. Few Brazilians could fail to agree that the political establishment could do with a cleaning; what worried them was just how far the new government would go, particularly in view of the people who were now doing the cleaning. They were a combination of two elements, the military and the right, which many Brazilians, to put it mildly, did not find exactly inspiring. Although they respected their new 'President', General Castelo Branco, in the same way as they had respected Gaspar Dutra in 1945, from the very start the new government was to give them plenty of food for reflection. Between April and June, 441 persons, many of whom seemed hardly to fit the description of subversive or corrupt, had their political rights withdrawn for ten years. They included six state governors, Janio Quadros and Juscelino Kubitscheck; the man who had built

Brasilia was now deprived even of the right to vote. In protest, his party, the PSD, withdrew its support of the government in Congress. But the Act which allowed the government to take this kind of action lapsed on 15 June and it was not extended by General Castelo Branco, despite the urgings of the army-directed investigating committee that it should remain in force for another four months. Several thousand people, however, had also been arrested, and without trial, on charges of subversion and Brazilians were again confronted with something they had thought they would never see again: the demoralizing spectacle of jails so overcrowded that many of those arrested had to be transferred to penal settlements which Vargas had once used, or detained in forts and even in prison ships. Later, however, those who had been detained for fifty days without being specifically charged were released. Yet in April 1965, one year after the new government had taken over, some 1,500 persons were still in jail.

Other constitutional amendments, designed to take some of the unpredictability out of politics, were submitted to and approved by Congress, even though some of them must have been hard to swallow for they reflected the suspicions the military in Brazil have always had of civilian politicians. They included the cancellation of the election due in 1964 and extended the Revolutionary government's term of office to 15 March 1967. Presidential elections would be held 120 days beforehand, at the same time as Congressional elections. A presidential candidate must also receive an absolute majority, otherwise Congress must confirm the election of the candidate with the largest number of votes. But the old ideal to extend the vote to the voiceless illiterate was once again rejected. The presidential and vice-presidential terms of office were reduced from five to four years and a candidate for vice-presidency would no longer be voted for independently. This practice had enabled men, like João Goulart, to figure in a government who often had views which were quite opposed to those of the president and the parties he represented. In future the vice-president would be automatically elected with the presidential candidate with whom he stood. All members of the armed forces from the rank of sergeant were also to be eligible for elected office and members of Congress were no longer immune from criminal proceedings. A further constitutional amendment trans, ferred to military tribunals trials of persons charged with treason, corruption or with crimes against political and social order.

No Brazilian government, apart from the Vargas dictatorship, had ever acquired such power, and much of it had been with the blessing of Congress. In 1965 despite the spectre of dictatorship or the pos, sible indefinite continuation of the present régime and uneasy feelings that those old bogies, the right-wing forces in the country and the mili, tary, were making sure that they would never be threatened again, a growing number of Brazilians supported Castelo Branco and his pursed-lip reformers. They realized that Brazil's ailments needed more than drugs, they called for surgery. Some even conceded ruefully that democracy had perhaps been used not so much as a tonic as an intoxicant.

Brazilians have been betrayed so often by those in whom they have voluntarily placed their trust that these new leaders whom they had accepted, or been forced to accept, as necessary, carried an even greater responsibility. Their aims could not be achieved simply by locking up communists and chasing other political 'undesirables' off the streets; they had already done perhaps too much of that. (In 1965 one of President Castelo Branco's personal problems was still how to contain the 'hard line' in his régime and in the army who were deter, mined to carry on with the witch hunt.) This government had to justify the authority it had exacted by show of arms and earn trust. And they still had to inspire Brazilians all over again, and not with dazzling promises. Brazilians, once they have elected a government, have tended to sit back waiting for it to perform miracles. Now they were being told that if they wanted prosperity they had to pull in their belts and not only work for it but make sacrifices too. Brazilians had heard such exhortations before but what was making them sit up with a jerk was the realization that this government meant what it said. And to prove it they continued to back up their words with more new legislation aimed at the heart of a number of sacred cows from tax evasion to wages and profits structures.

In 1965 some of these policies were already producing results.

Inflation had not been halted but the pace had slowed down. Once again foreign investors were showing a renewed, if cautious, interest in Brazil's fortunes. Far greater American aid, too, now seemed assured, for the Castelo Branco administration was the sort of govern, ment, strong, but moderate enough not to arouse dangerous anta, gonism and, above all, unequivocally intolerant of communism, which the Americans hoped to see setting a pattern for other Latin American countries. But the ordinary Brazilian voter had still to be inspired. In the elections for state governors in October 1965, the first public test of the new régime, some notable supporters of its ideals were defeated. Earlier, former President Kubitscheck, outlawed for alleged financial and administrative irresponsibility verging on out, right corruption, had returned to Brazil and received a delirious public welcome. It was *his* supporters that many Brazilians enthusi, astically elected in October 1965. The question which President Castelo Branco and even his more restrained reformers now faced was this. If presidential elections were held as promised in 1966, could the mass of the electorate be trusted not to return to power the same political forces which had done so much damage, certainly to Brazil's credit? The 'hard liners' who had opposed the October elections had no doubt at all. Brazilians clamour for an effective government. Ironically, it seemed unlikely that they would get one in a democracy, at least for the time being.

The greatest challenge to this government, and its eventual successors, was how to instil a new mentality in the Brazilians and a new attitude towards each other and to the world around them. Only to look into Brazil's history and the temperament of her people was to realize just how great, and very likely, heart, breaking for many, the task would be. How to bring cohesion to this vast land of unexplored wealth: two divided worlds, not only in terms of material and social advancement but mentally, and to give a new sense of destiny to a country which has remained for so long on the verge of fulfilling its promise and justifying nature's bounty; that is the challenge, the adventure of Brazil.

Notes on the Text

2 THE TWO BRAZILS

1 From R. Morse, *Community to Metropolis*, Florida, 1958

3 THE OUTLINE OF THE PAST

2 See Bibliography

4 THE FRAME OF THE FUTURE. INDEPENDENCE

3 Pedro I's letters to his father, Dom João VI. Archives of the Imprensa Nacional, Lisbon
4 See C. H. Haring, *Empire in Brazil*, Harvard, 1958
5 See S. C. da Costa, *Every Inch a King*, New York, 1950

5 THE EMPIRE AND THE OTHER PEDRO

6 See M. W. Williams, *Dom Pedro the Magnanimous*, South Carolina, 1937

8 THE BRAZILIAN

7 See Bibliography
8 See *Brasil*, Statistical Review published annually by the Ministry of Foreign Affairs (Anúario Estatistico do Brasil)

9 THE FACES OF CULTURE

9 See G. Freyre, *Brazil – an Interpretation*, New York, 1945, p 155
10 See S. Putnam, *Marvellous Journey, A Survey of Four Centuries of Brazilian Writing*, New York, 1948
11 See M. L. A. Silva, *Galeria*, Rio de Janeiro, 1954
12 See H. Mindlin, *Modern Architecture in Brazil*, New York, 1956

13 The plan derived its name from the initial letters of the words: Saude (health); Alimentacão (food); Transporte (transport); and Energia (power)

List of Abbreviations

BNDE	National Economic Development Bank, Brazil
CSN	National Steel Company, Brazil
IBC	Brazilian Coffee Institute
Icap	Inter-American Committee for the Alliance for Progress
Lafta	Latin American Free Trade Association or Area
OAS	Organization of American States
OECD	Organization for Economic Co-operation and Development
PSB	Brazilian Socialist Party
PSD	Social Democratic Party
PSP	Social Progressive Party
PTB	Brazilian Labour Party
SUDENE	Northeast Development Authority, Brazil
UDN	National Democratic Union

Select Bibliography

ARCHITECTURE

Mindlin, H., *Modern Architecture in Brazil*, New York, 1956
Goodwin, P. L., *Brazil Builds. Architecture, New and Old, 1652–1942*, New York, Museum of Modern Art, 1943

CULTURE

Azevedo, F. de, *Brazilian Culture*, New York, 1950
Putnam, S., *Marvellous Journey, A Survey of Four Centuries of Brazilian Writing*, New York, 1948

ECONOMY

Furtado, C., *The Economic Growth of Brazil: A Survey from Colonial to Modern Times*, London and Los Angeles, 1963
Hirschman, A. O., *Journeys Towards Progress, Studies of Economic Policy Making in Latin America*, New York, 1963

HISTORY

Freyre, G. (trans. and ed. by H. de Onís), *The Mansions and the Shanties: The Making of Modern Brazil*, New York, 1963
Southey, R., *History of Brazil*, 3 vols, London, 1810–19
Armitage, J., *The History of Brazil*, 2 vols, London, 1836
Calógeras, J. P., *A History of Brazil*, North Carolina, 1939
Costa, S. C. da, *Every Inch a King*, New York, 1950
Williams, M. W., *Dom Pedro the Magnanimous*, South Carolina, 1937
Boxer, C. R., *The Golden Age of Brazil, 1695–1750*, London and Los Angeles, 1962

POLITICS

T. L. Smith, *Brazil: People and Institutions* (rev. ed.), Louisiana, 1963
C. Wagley, *An Introduction to Brazil*, New York and London, 1963
E. Dell, *Brazil: The Dilemma of Reform*, London, The Fabian Society, 1964
C. H. Haring, *Empire in Brazil: A New World Experiment with Monarchy*, Harvard, 1958

GENERAL

Freyre, G., *Brazil – an Interpretation*, New York, 1945
Cunha, E. da (trans. by S. Putnam), *Rebellion in the Backlands (Os Sertões)*, Chicago, 1957
Konrad, G. (trans. by B. Miall), *A Naturalist in Brazil. The Flora and Fauna and the People of Brazil*, London, 1931
Pierson, D., *Negroes in Brazil, a Study of Race Contact at Bahia*, Chicago, 1942
Zweig, S., *Brazil, Land of the Future*, London, 1942
Webster, C. K., *Britain and the Independence of Latin America*, London, 1938
Manchester, A. K., *British Pre-eminence in Brazil. Its rise and decline*, North Carolina, 1933
Seitz, G. (trans. by A. J. Pomerans), *People of the Rain-Forests*, London, 1963
Bates, H. W., *The Naturalist on the River Amazon*, London and Los Angeles, 1962

Who's Who

ALBUQUERQUE, Julio Prestes de (known as Julio Prestes) (1882–1946). Born São Paulo. Elected president in 1929 but prevented from taking office by the Vargas revolution of 1930.

ANCHIETA, Father José de (1534–91). Spanish Jesuit missionary who came to Brazil in 1553 at the age of nineteen. A teacher responsible for laying the foundations of peace between Indians and settlers in the region known today as São Paulo.

ANDRADA, José Bonifacio Ribeiro de Andrada Machado e Silva (known as José Bonifacio) (1763–1838). Born Santos, state of São Paulo. Known as the Father of Brazil's independence. As a major he fought with the Portuguese troops under Wellington in the Peninsular War. Returned to Brazil in 1819 and joined the movement for independence. He exercised considerable influence on Dom Pedro, the Prince Regent. Although not a politician, Bonifacio became one of the most influential liberal statesmen of the new Empire. This liberal outlook eventually brought him into open conflict with Pedro I, and in 1823 he was banished from Brazil, remaining in exile for six years. Nevertheless, when Pedro I abdicated in 1831 he named Bonifacio as his son's guardian who was to be crowned Pedro II in 1840.

BARBOSA, Rui (1849–1924). Born Bahia. Lawyer, journalist, writer and states- man. One of the great idealists of Brazil at the turn of the nineteenth century and a fearless exponent of liberal thought. In Parliament and in the press he was one of the most articulate campaigners against slavery. An ardent republican, he was soon to become an opponent of the first republican government – in which he was Minister of Finance – because of its militarist tendencies. Even- tually forced into exile, he went to England. He returned to Brazil in 1895, entered the Senate, where he remained until his death. He was one of the principal authors of Brazil's civil code and many of his pronouncements on legal and constitutional issues have passed into Brazilian textbooks.

213

BARROS, Adhemar Pereira de, b. 1901. Born Piracicaba, São Paulo. Began his career as a doctor. Entered politics in 1934 when he became São Paulo's State Deputy. Was appointed Governor of the state of São Paulo by Getulio Vargas (1938–41). Afterwards was twice elected Governor of the state of São Paulo and played a prominent part in the revolt against the left-wing government of President Goulart in 1964. At present leader of the left-wing Social Progressive Party. He has always been essentially a populist leader and a rather unorthodox and flamboyant figure. He built up a considerable personal fortune and has wide business interests in industry and farming. He also has an impressive record of administrative achievements and is responsible for some of the largest building projects in the state of São Paulo, including schools, hospitals and roads. He has twice (1955, 1960) stood as candidate for the presidency of the Republic.

BERNARDES, Arthur da Silva (known as Arthur Bernardes) (1875–1955). Born Minas Gerais. President, 1922–6.

BRAZ, Wenceslão Braz Pereira Gomes (known as Wenceslão Braz), b. 1868. Born Minas Gerais. President, 1914–17.

CABRAL, Admiral Pedro Alvares (c. 1466–1519). Born Belmonte, Portugal. The discoverer of Brazil. Son of a government official, his family had close connexions with the Portuguese Court. Nevertheless, after his return from Brazil he became a victim of intrigue and resigned his post. He received little recognition from his contemporaries and his remains were discovered by a Brazilian historian, Varnhagem (1816–78) in a convent in Santarem, where they had lain forgotten for over 300 years.

CAMPOS, Roberto de Oliveira, b. 1917. Born in Cuiabá, Mato Grosso. Minister for Planning and Economic Co-ordination in the Castelo Branco government. Entered the Brazilian Foreign Service in 1939; was Second Secretary at the Brazilian Embassy in Washington (1942–6); Secretary to the Brazilian Delegation at the Bretton Woods Conference in 1944; Brazilian Representative at the International Council for Emergency Food Supplies in 1945; Economic Counsellor to the permanent Brazilian Delegation at the United Nations Organization, 1947–59; Economic Counsellor of the Brazilian Delegation to the V, VI, VII, VIII and IX Sessions of the Social and Economic Councils of the 2nd, 3rd and 4th Sessions of the General Assembly of the United Nations, 1947–9; Economic Counsellor to the Brazilian Delegation at the International Conference on Commerce and Labour, held in

Havana in 1948; Secretary to the Consultative Committee of Commercial Agreements of the Ministry of Foreign Affairs in 1951; Economic Counsellor of the Brazilian Delegation and the 4th Consultative Assembly of Foreign Ministers of the American Republics, held in Washington in 1951; Economic Counsellor of the Brazilian Section of the Brazil-USA Commission for Economic Development, 1951–2. He is also Assistant Professor of Economics at the University of Brazil; Director General of the National Economic Development Bank; Consultant to the Council of Development of the Presidency of the Republic in 1956; was appointed Ambassador to Washington in 1961.

CAMPOS SALLES, Manoel Ferraz de (known as Campos Salles) (1841–1913). Born São Paulo. President, 1898–1902.

CASTELO BRANCO, General Humberto Alencar, b. 1900. Born in Ceará. Entered the army at the age of seventeen and rose to the rank of General in 1952. He was one of the commanders of the Brazilian Expeditionary Force which fought in Italy during the Second World War. He took part in the revolt against the Goulart government in 1964. In May of that year he was elected President of the Republic by an overwhelming majority in Congress, securing 361 votes. His nearest rival received 3.

CASTRO ALVES, Antonio (1847–71). Born Bahia. A poet who devoted much of his life to the abolitionist campaign. Became known as the Poet of the Slaves and his impassioned poems profoundly influenced public opinion against the institution of slavery.

CAXIAS, Duke of. See LIMA E SILVA, Luiz Alves.

CHATEAUBRIAND, Assis (Assis Chateaubriand Bandeira de Mello), b. 1892. Born Umbuzeiro, Paraiba. Journalist, politician and diplomat. Started life as a lawyer and became Professor at the Faculty of Law, Recife. Founded Diarios Associados. He owns over thirty newspapers and magazines and many radio and television stations and a news agency; was elected to the Federal Senate; is also a patron of the arts, thanks to his initiative the now internationally known Museum of Modern Art in São Paulo was founded. In 1956 he was elected to the Brazilian Academy. In 1953 he visited Great Britain as a member of the Brazilian Delegation to the Coronation of H M Queen Elizabeth II. Was Ambassador to London (1957–61).

COCHRANE, Lord. See DUNDONALD, Thomas Cochrane, 10th Earl of.

COSTA LISBOA, Antonio Francisco da, *Aleijadinho* (1730–1814). Sculptor. Born Ouro Prêto, state of Minas Gerais, illegitimate son of a Portuguese carpenter, his mother was a Negro slave. In his forties he contracted leprosy, yet it was in the latter half of his life, when his body had become hideously deformed and he could only move by crawling on his knees and the stumps of his arms, that he began to produce his often strikingly beautiful sculptures and carvings which decorate the churches of Ouro Prêto, many of which have become national monuments to his unique art.

COSTA, Lúcio, b. 1902. Born Toulouse, France. One of the major influences in modern Brazilian architecture; was the designer of the new capital, Brasilia.

CRUZ, Oswaldo Gonçalves (1872–1917). Born São Luis de Piraitinga, state of São Paulo. Scientist. He began life as a general practitioner; studied at the Pasteur Institute in Paris (1896–9); returning to Brazil he resumed his general practice in one of the poorer quarters of Rio de Janeiro where he lived. In 1900 the Brazilian health authorities appealed to the Pasteur Institute to send them a French scientist to direct the newly created Manguinhos Research Institute in Rio. The Institute recommended Oswaldo Cruz and he was duly appointed. In 1903 he became Director of Public Health in the Rodrigues Alves government and began his long and successful campaign – despite often bitter opposition to his methods – to rid Rio of yellow fever.

CUNHA, Leitão da, b. 1903. Minister of Foreign Affairs in the Castelo Branco government; graduate of the University of Rio de Janeiro; entered the Foreign Service 1929. During the Second World War was Brazil's representative at Allied Headquarters and the Free French government until 1944; minister plenipotentiary since 1943, was Consul-General, then Chargé d'Affaires in Rome until 1945. Consul in Geneva until 1946, during which time he was a delegate to the Preparatory Commission of the UN in London; has represented Brazil on the Balkan Commission of the UN; was a national delegate to the VI Assembly of the UN until 1952; Head of the Political and Cultural Department of the Brazilian Ministry of Foreign Affairs until 1953 and Secretary-General of the Ministry until 1954; Ambassador to Brussels (1956); Ambassador to Cuba (1956–61); represented Brazil at the IV Meeting of American Foreign Ministers held in Costa Rica in 1960.

DUNDONALD, Thomas Cochrane, 10th Earl of (1775–1860). Remembered in South America, particularly in Chile and Brazil, for his help in their struggles for independence. In 1817 he was commissioned by Chile to command her navy in the war of independence against Spain. From 1823 to 1825 he transferred his services to Brazil, commanding part of the Brazilian navy which put down the last resistance of the Portuguese in Brazil to independence from Portugal.

DUTRA, Marshall Eurico Gaspar, b. 1885. Born Cuiabá, Mato Grosso. President (1945–51) after the overthrow of the Vargas dictatorship.

EU, Luiz-Felippe-Maria-Fernando-Gastão de Orleans, Marshal, Prince, Count d'Eu (1842–1922). Son of the Duke of Nemours and grandson of King Louis Philippe. Married Princess Isabel, daughter of Pedro II, of Brazil.

FONSECA, Marshal Hermes Rodrigues da (1855–1923). Born Rio Grande do Sul. Nephew of Deodoro da Fonseca, founder of the Republic. President, 1910–14.

FONSECA, Marshal Manoel Deodoro da (1827–1892). Born Alagôas. Was the central figure in the movement which overthrew Pedro II and established the Republic in 1889. Brazil's first president, 1889–91.

FREYRE, Professor Gilberto, b. 1900. Brazil's foremost sociologist, a field in which he has also attained international recognition. Director of the Institute of Social Studies at the University of Recife. Received an honorary Doctorate of Letters from Sussex University, 1965. Among his best-known works translated into English are: The Masters & The Slaves and The Mansions & The Shanties.

FURTADO, Celso, b. 1920. Minister of Planning and Economic Development in the Goulart government. He took his degree in law at the University of Brazil and studied in Paris and Cambridge, England. He has held a number of important posts: Head of the Development Division of the Economic Commission for Latin America; Director of the Brazilian National Economic Development Bank, BNDE; was Director of the technical studies which were the basis of new development plans for the Brazilian northeast and was executive Director of the Development Council for the Northeast and Superintendent of the Northeast Development Authority, SUDENE. After the revolution of 1964 he was deprived of his political rights for ten years and took up the post of visiting professor in the Department of Economics at Yale University.

GOMES, Antonio Carlos (1837–96). Born Campinas, state of São Paulo. Son of a tailor and part-time musician, Carlos Gomes played in the local brass band. At twenty-two he left home to pursue his musical career in Rio de Janeiro. He was almost destitute when he attracted the attention of Pedro II, who became his patron and later sent him to study in Italy. His best-known operas are Il

Guaraní; Escravo. His last opera, O *Condor,* was produced at La Scala Milan in 1891.

GOULART, João Belchior Marques, b. 1918. Born São Borja, Rio Grande do Sul. In 1945 he became a member of the newly formed Brazilian Labour Party and was elected president of the Regional Headquarters. In the same year he was elected State Deputy and joined in the campaign for the election in 1950 of Getulio Vargas. During the Vargas government he became Federal Deputy and eventually president of the Brazilian Labour Party. In 1953 he was appointed Minister of Labour but was obliged to resign in 1954 in the face of protests against his demagogy. In 1955 he was elected vice-president of the Republic. He was again elected vice-president in 1960 and, as vice-president in the Janio Quadros government, became president in August 1961 on Quadros's resignation. Throughout his political life he had been distrusted as a demagogue with excessive leanings towards the extreme left. In April 1964 he was deposed on the charges of subversion and corruption but escaped into exile to Uruguay.

ISABEL, Princess Dona Isabel, Christina, Leopoldina, Augusta, Michaela, Gabriela, Raphaela, Gonzaga (1846–1921). Born Rio de Janeiro. Daughter of Pedro II, Second Emperor of Brazil. Regent on three occasions during her father's travels in Europe. Like her father, an ardent abolitionist and, as Regent, signed some of the laws which finally abolished slavery in Brazil. Married Marshal Prince Count d'Eu (*q.v.*).

JÔAO VI, Dom (1767–1826). 27th King of Portugal, first King of the United Kingdom of Portugal, Brazil and the Algarves, Emperor of Brazil, father of Pedro I, proclaimer of Brazil's independence. On the invasion of Portugal during the Napoleonic War, Jôao VI, then Regent, took refuge in Brazil in 1808, accompanied by almost the entire Portuguese Court. Rio de Janeiro became the seat of the Portuguese Empire. Returned to Portugal in 1821 leaving his son, Pedro, as Regent. Jôao VI signed the Treaty of Recognition of Brazil's independence on 29 August 1825.

KUBITSCHECK DE OLIVEIRA, Juscelino, b. 1902. Born Minas Gerais. President (1956–61). Of Czech origin on his mother's side; his father died when he was one year old, leaving the family almost destitute. The upbringing of the family fell entirely on his mother, a schoolteacher. Her ambition was that her son should become a doctor. As a young man he worked as a telegraph clerk by night so that he could study by day. He took his degree in medicine and went on to become a surgeon. He entered politics in 1933 and a year later was elected State Deputy for Minas Gerais. In 1937 he abandoned politics and resumed his practice. In 1939 he was appointed Mayor of Belo Horizonte and initiated a number of notable building and social security projects. In 1946 was elected to the National Assembly and in 1950 was elected Governor of Minas Gerais; He carried on and expanded the projects initiated when he was mayor. He also successfully attracted new industries to the state, which marked the positive beginning of the industrial development of Minas Gerais. Elected president in 1955, he took office on 31 January the following year. His slogan was: Fifty Years Progress in Five; the industrialization of Brazil and the attracting of foreign industries and capital on a hitherto unprecedented scale was a prime concern of his government. He began the building of Brasilia, the new capital, which he inaugurated in April 1960, just before his term of office ended. Regarded as the strongest candidate for the presidency in the election of 1964, which was cancelled by the revolt against the Goulart government in that year. The new government deprived him of his political rights for ten years and he went into voluntary exile in Portugal. In the event of a free election, Kubitscheck is still considered to be a strong candidate for presidency.

LACERDA, Carlos, b. 1914. Born Rio de Janeiro. Journalist, political crusader; first Governor of the newly created (1960) state of Guanabára, which includes Rio de Janeiro, the former capital. Began life as a journalist. A leader of the National Democratic Union Party (UDN), he has been State Deputy and Senator. He is best known, however, for his violent crusades against political corruption and government ineptitude. He founded the Rio newspaper, *Tribuna da Imprensa*. His attacks on the Vargas government led to the attempt on his life in August 1954 and the ensuing scandal brought about the downfall of the government and Vargas's suicide. He has been the severest fault-finder of successive governments. As a young man he was for a short time a member of the Communist Party; from this he swung to the almost extreme right. He was one of the leading civilian figures in the 1964 revolution which overthrew the Goulart government. He has since criticized the Castelo Branco government, particularly its economic policies. By the end of 1964 he launched his own campaign for the presidency of the Republic in the elections scheduled to be held in 1966. He is a devout Catholic.

LIMA E SILVA, Duke of Caxias, Luis Alves de (1803–80). Born Rio de Janeiro. The Father of the Brazilian Army; was created a Duke by Pedro II for his conduct of the war against Paraguay (1865–70) and in recognition of the role he played in the reorganization of Brazil's army.

MATARAZZO, Count Francisco (1854–1937). Born Castellabate, Italy. Founder of the largest industrial, business and finance empire in Latin America. He emigrated to Brazil as a young man and started a small grocery business in São Paulo. Later he opened a sausage and lard factory which expanded into a vast consortium of over seventy undertakings from manufacturing to finance houses and shipping which today employ over 20,000 people and still controlled by his family. He was awarded the papal title of Count by Pope Pius XII.

MAUÁ, Irineu Evangelista de Souza, Baron, then Viscount, Mauá (1813–89). Born Rio Grande do Sul, started life as a shop assistant at the age of eleven. Almost entirely self-educated, he became one of the most influential Brazilian financiers and industrialists of his time. Inspired the building of the first railways in Brazil, including the São Paulo railway.

MORAES BARROS, Prudente José de (known as Prudente de Moraes) (1841–1902). Born São Paulo. Brazil's first civilian president, 1894–6.

NIEMEYER, Oscar, b. 1907. Born Rio de Janeiro. One of Brazil's foremost architects. His work includes the Ministry of Education building in Rio de Janeiro, one of the most notable examples of modern Brazilian architecture (which he built in collaboration with Lucio Costa and with Le Corbusier as consultant), and the church at Pampulha near Belo Horizonte, a striking architectural experiment with murals by Cândido Portinari but which the church authorities refused to consecrate. Niemeyer was also responsible for some of the more revolutionary buildings in Brasilia, including the cathedral which is built partly underground. Was awarded the Lenin Peace Prize in 1963.

NÓBREGA, Father Manuel da (1517–70). Born Sinfães do Douro, Portugal. Jesuit missionary who came to Brazil in 1549. Devoted his years in Brazil to the conversion of the Indians; fought fearlessly to protect them from slavery and to provide them with some form of education. On both counts he met bitter opposition from the Portuguese settlers. Was the founder of some of the first schools in the colony.

PEDRO I, Dom Pedro de Alcantara Francisco Antonio João Carlos Xavier de Paula Miguel Raphael Joaquim José Gonzaga Paschoal Cypriano Seraphim de Bragança e Bourbon (1798–1834). First Emperor of Brazil. Declared Brazil's independence on 7 September 1822 and crowned Emperor of Brazil on 1 December 1822. Successor to the Portuguese throne, he abdicated in favour of his daughter, Maria da Gloria, who was to be crowned Queen Maria II. Abdicated the throne of Brazil in 1831, in favour of his five-year-old son, Pedro d'Alcantara.

PEDRO II, Dom Pedro d'Alcantara-João-Carlos-Leopoldo-Salvador-Bibiano-Francisco-Xavier-de-Paula-Leocadio-Miguel-Gabriel-Raphael-Gonzaga (1825-91). Second and last Emperor of Brazil. Born Rio de Janeiro. In an attempt to bring unity to the country in the stormy Regency period (1831-40) which followed Pedro I's abdication, Pedro d'Alcantara, although barely sixteen, was declared of age on 23 July 1840. He ruled Brazil until the Empire was overthrown in 1889.

PEIXOTO, Marshal Floriano Viera (1839-95). Born Alagôas, was the first vice-president of the Republic. Assumed the office of president (1891-4) on the resignation of Deodoro da Fonseca, the first president. Both men had been leaders of the movement which overthrew the Brazilian Empire in 1889.

PENA or PENNA, Afonso Augusto Moreira (known as Afonso Pena) (1847-1909). Born Minas Gerais. President, 1906-9.

PESSÔA, Epitacio da Silva (known as Epitacio Pessôa) (1865-1942). Born Paraiba do Norte. President, 1919-22.

PORTINARI, Cândido (1903-62). Born Brodósqui, São Paulo. Brazil's foremost and most influential modern painter. His works include the monumental mural 'War and Peace' at the United Nations headquarters in New York.

PRESTES, Luis Carlos, b. 1898. Born Pôrto Alégre, Rio Grande do Sul. One of the founders and still one of the most influential leaders of the Brazilian communist movement. He began his career in the army which he abandoned in 1924 to devote himself to revolutionary activities. Exiled and imprisoned on several occasions; in 1945 he was elected a senator. His mandate was withdrawn in 1947 when the Communist Party was outlawed. Although theoretically wanted on charges of subversion, his personal prestige allowed him a great measure of freedom in later years when he became far less militant.

QUADROS, Janio, b. 1917. Born Mato Grosso. President, 31.1.1961-25.8.1961. Began life as a schoolmaster; entered politics in 1947; was elected member of the São Paulo Municipality and later State Deputy. In 1953, at the age of thirty-six, he was elected Mayor of São Paulo with a 70 per cent majority. In October 1954 he was elected State Governor; in 1960 he was elected President of the Republic, receiving over 48 per cent of the vote, the highest majority ever achieved by a Brazilian president. Took office in January 1961; resigned August 1961 in protest against what he described as the hampering tactics of Congress. After the revolution of 1964 was deprived of his political rights for ten years; but a year later there was evidence that he was again exercising influence behind the scenes, particularly in São Paulo, electorally one of the most important of the Brazilian states. His supporters confidently predict that he will one day return as Governor of São Paulo and eventually perhaps even as President of the Republic. A moderate left-winger, Quadros has always been a rebel against the Establishment, but has consistently refused to be committed to any party. His political independence and brilliant administrative record and reputation for integrity as Governor of São Paulo are still his strongest appeal to ordinary Brazilians.

RIO BRANCO, José Maria da Silva Paranhos, Baron (1845–1912). Born Rio de Janeiro. The son of Viscount Rio Branco and a major figure in Brazil's diplomatic history. During his long association with the Brazilian Ministry of Foreign Affairs he was largely responsible for laying the foundations of Brazilian foreign policy.

RIO BRANCO, José Maria da Silva Paranhos, Viscount (1819–80). Born Bahia. One of the most influential statesmen during the reign of Pedro II. Was a prominent figure in the campaign for the abolition of slavery.

RODRIGUES ALVES, Francisco de Paula (known as Rodrigues Alves) (1848–1919). Born São Paulo. President, 1902–6. Was elected again in 1918 but died before he could take office.

RONDON, General Cândido Mariano da Silva (1865–1958). Born in Cuiabá, Mato Grosso. He entered the army and first achieved prominence when in 1890 he was chosen to lead an expedition to lay 400 miles of telegraph wire through the jungle of central Brazil. In ten years he and his party laid 2,000 miles, often through country in which no white man had ever penetrated. This work brought him his first contact with the primitive Indian communities of Mato Grosso and he devoted the rest of his life, not only to making peace with the Indians but to bringing some measure of civilization to these remote regions. In 1910 he created the Indian Protection Service. One of the rules he imposed, and which is still observed by members of the Service, was that in Indian country they should always travel unarmed. Rondon's explorations made Brazilians even more aware of the great wealth of natural resources which existed in this wilderness of the heart of Brazil. Rondon also acted as guide to former President Theodore Roosevelt on his expedition into central Brazil in 1913.

SIMONSEN, Roberto Cochrane (1889–1948). Born Santos. A descendant of Lord Cochrane (q.v.). An engineer, he became one of the leading businessmen and industrialists of the late nineteenth century. Was a founder of the Brazilian cotton industry and a pioneer of social services in the early 1940s during the Vargas régime.

SOUZA, Washington Luiz Pereira (known as Washington Luiz) (1870–1957). Born Rio de Janeiro but spent most of his life in São Paulo. President, 1926–30. Deposed by the Vargas revolution.

SUSSEKIND, Arnaldo Lopes, b. 1917. Born Rio de Janeiro. Minister of Labour and Social Services in the Castelo Branco government. A lawyer, he has become one of Brazil's greatest authorities on labour and social legislation. President of the Permanent Commission of Social Rights of the Ministry of Labour; Professor of the Brazilian Law Faculty; active member of the International Labour Organization; was Attorney-General for the Ministry of Labour in the Janio Quadros government. He is the author of many books on social legislation.

TIRADENTES. *See* XAVIER, Joaquim José da Silva.

VARGAS, Getulio Dornelles (1883–1954). Born São Borja, Rio Grande do Sul. Head of the provisional government 1930–4; President 1934–7; Dictator 1937–45; President 1951–4.

VILLA-LOBOS, Heitor (1887–1959). Born Rio de Janeiro. Brazil's foremost composer and regarded as the creator of the nationalist movement in Brazilian music.

XAVIER, Joaquim José da Silva, *Tiradentes* (1748–92). Born Minas Gerais. In 1789 was the leader of the first organized movement for independence. The conspiracy was betrayed and he was hanged in 1792. Xavier had been a dentist, hence his nickname, *Tiradentes*, the toothpuller.

Acknowledgements

Associated Press Ltd, 48, 82;

from F. Biard, *Deux Années au Brésil*, Paris, 1862, by kind permission of F. R. Cowell, 32;

by courtesy of the Brazilian Embassy, 2, 3, 4, 8, 10, 11, 13, 14, 15, 23, 29, 40, 42, 43, 44, 52, 54, 55, 58, 59, 60, 62, 65, 66, 67, 68, (P. Scheir) 69, 70, 72, 73, 74, 75; A.C.L. Bruxelles, 63;

from T de Bry, *Brasilia durch J. Staden*, Frankfurt, 1593, by courtesy of the Trustees of the British Museum, 17, 18, 19;

Camera Press Ltd., 49, (*O Cruzeiro*) 85, 89, 90, 91, 92;

Crown Copyright, 79;

from J. B. Debret, *Voyage pittoresque et historique au Brésil*, Paris, 1834-9, by courtesy of the Trustees of the British Museum, 24, 25, 26;

Esso Standard Ltd, 51, 56, 61;

by kind permission of G. H. Green, Librarian of Canning House, London, 21, 22, 30, 31, 34, 35, 39, 41, 50;

from A. Heulhard, *Villegagnon, roi d'Amérique: un homme de mer au XVIe siècle, 1510-1572*, Paris, 1897, by courtesy of the Trustees of the British Museum, 20;

Keystone Press Agency, 77, 78, 80, 81, 86;

from D. P. Kidder and J. C. Fletcher, *Brazil and the Brazilians*, London, 1857, by courtesy of Canning House Library, 28, 38;

from *Livro das Armadas* by courtesy of C. A. G. Estorninho, The British Council, Lisbon, 16;

H. Mann, 1, 9, 46, 64, 76;

Paul Popper Ltd, 5;

Presna Latina, 71, 87, 88;

P. Suschitzky, 7, 12, 45, 47, 93;

United Press International (UK) Ltd, 83, 84;

from F. R. Walsh, *Notices of Brazil*, Vol. II, London, 1830, by courtesy of Canning House Library, 33, 36, 37;

World Health Organization (L. Nadel), 57.

Index

228